Knowing God's Love

John D. LaBarbara

Knowing God's Love

❖

Eight Essential Truths
Every Catholic Should Know

SOPHIA INSTITUTE PRESS
Manchester, New Hampshire

Sophia Institute Press
Box 5284, Manchester, NH 03108
1-800-888-9344

www.SophiaInstitute.com

Sophia Institute Press® is a registered trademark of Sophia Institute.

Library of Congress Cataloging-in-Publication Data

Names: LaBarbara, John D., author.
Title: Knowing God's love : eight essential truths that every Catholic should know / John D. LaBarbara.
Description: Manchester, New Hampshire : Sophia Institute Press, 2016. | Includes bibliographical references.
Identifiers: LCCN 2016033645 | ISBN 9781622823499 (pbk. : alk. paper)
Subjects: LCSH: God (Christianity) — Love. | Love — Religious aspects — Catholic Church. | Catholic Church — Doctrines.
Classification: LCC BT140 .L33 2016 | DDC 231/.6 — dc23 LC record available at https://lccn.loc.gov/2016033645

First printing

Contents

Foreword, by Curtis A. Martin. vii

Preface ix

Acknowledgments. xi

Introduction: The Ultimate Question 3

Part I
The Foundational Truths

1. God Is Love. 7
   There is only one God, but God is in fact a "We," the
   Holy Trinity, who is the very definition of love.

2. Man Is Created in God's Image 13
   Each person is created as a reflection of God's love, and
   we best reflect that image when we are in communion, in
   marriage, or in friendship.

3. God Desires Us. 29
   God is a "We," and He desires us to enter into this deep
   love of the Trinity through the communion of the Church.

Part II
The Foundational Truths Applied Personally

4. To Work Is to Share in God's Creation 49
   God begins His creation by working, and we are also given
   the gift to work and to be part of God's loving, creative
   act.

5. Charity Is Required to Love God and Man. 63
   God is love, and we must reflect that love to others in
   charity, but charity must also be effective.

6. Catholic Social Teaching Is Rooted in Truth 81
   Our acts of charity ought to be based on love and truth,
   and we should always be ready to adjust our methods to do
   the greatest good we can for our neighbor.

Part III
The Foundational Truths Applied Publicly

7. Governing Requires Prudence
   for Real Charity to Occur. 95
   The proper role of government is to promote safety and
   security in order for people to work, to give, and to choose
   to help others without fear.

8. We Are Responsible for Reflecting
   God's Love in Public Life. 117
   Our responsibility in society and in politics is actively to
   support candidates, politicians, and policies that best pro-
   mote the common good and allow for the practice of real
   charity.

Conclusion: Knowing Love 147

About the Author. 157

Foreword

Although there are many great Catholic scholars and theologians who write effectively on Scripture, the *Catechism*, and the magisterial documents of the Church, John LaBarbara's genius is his ability to synthesize them in such a complete, compelling, and applicable way. That's why I encouraged him to write this book.

John's zeal for the truths of the Faith and his passion for evangelization come from decades of unique experiences and insights that resonate with readers from cradle Catholics to potential converts. Raised as a Protestant, John developed a passion for Sacred Scripture that prompted him to pursue theology at Simpson University and, after graduating summa cum laude, to continue his study of New Testament Greek at Fuller Seminary.

What struck me as a virtue of this work is how well John integrates the vast number of excellent sources from which he draws—especially his command of Sacred Scripture. This work serves as a ready resource, a "where to go" to find the Church's voice on these all important subjects. Most Catholics have a notion that the Church has something to say on any given issue, but they don't know where to go for the answers. John has done a great job of compiling these answers in an engaging, readily accessible, and inspiring way.

Inspired by the example of Pope St. John Paul II's Theology of the Body, John succinctly and with great clarity unpacks Catholic social teaching from the foundational truths about creation and personal dignity. As an example, his chapters on charity and social teaching offer something I believe every Catholic needs to hear.

Similarly, in his chapter "Our Crucial Responsibility in Politics and Society," John synthesizes the Church's key teachings on these matters from nearly half a dozen magisterial writings and clearly shows how they can be applied—removing much of the confusion so many Catholics suffer from in regard to these vital issues. It is both timely and compelling.

John clearly shows the Church's teachings on each of these critical topics, from the Church's own magisterial source documents. Equally important, John demonstrates *why* the Church teaches what she does on each one and how these teachings fit together perfectly in a true unity of faith and truth.

—Curtis A. Martin
Founder, Fellowship of Catholic
University Students (FOCUS)

Preface

The purpose of this book is to equip Catholics for the New Evangelization by giving them the Church's teachings—from her own magisterial documents—in an accessible way that is simple to apply and easy to share. To that end, each chapter concludes with a short, bullet-point summary of the main points covered within it.

This foundational approach to apologetics is in response to St. Peter's admonition:

Always be prepared to give an answer to anyone who asks you the reason for the hope that is within you. But do this with gentleness and respect. (1 Pet. 3:15, NIV)

It is also based on two convictions. The first is that it's not our job to convert anyone to the Catholic Faith—that is the Holy Spirit's job:

And when he is come, he [the Holy Spirit] will convince the world of sin, and of righteousness, and of judgment. (John 16:8, DR)

The second was expressed by Fulton Sheen as follows:

There are not over a hundred people in the United States who hate the Catholic Church. There are millions, however, who hate what they wrongly believe to be the Catholic Church—which is, of course, quite a different thing.[1]

That was certainly my experience journeying into the Church. The same pattern repeated itself over and over again. First, I would learn that what I thought the Church taught was not at all what she actually taught. Then, gradually, I would see the reasonableness of what she did teach, primarily through the Scriptures. Next, the Holy Spirit would convince me of the truth of what I had learned. Through this process He led me, a former Evangelical Protestant, into the Church. My prayer is that this book will equip you to help others follow the same route.

---

[1] Archbishop Fulton J. Sheen, preface to *Radio Replies*, vol. 1, http://www.radioreplies.info/vol-1-preface.php.

Acknowledgments

My thanks to those who played critical roles in my coming into the Catholic Faith: Bryan Kelso, Bishop Michael Sheridan, and Archbishop Charles Chaput.

To those who played critical roles in my coming to work at the Augustine Institute and the Denver Catholic Biblical School: Dr. Tim Gray, Dr. Ben Akers, Dr. Ted Sri, and Dr. Jonathon Reyes.

To those who played a critical role in the writing of this book: Curtis Martin, Sarah O'Brien, Helena Scott, and all of my dedicated and faithful students at the Denver Catholic Biblical and Catechetical Schools.

To those who played critical roles in the publishing of this book: Dan Burke, Charlie McKinney, Michael Lichens, and Dr. Dan Cooper.

And especially to those who played critical roles in all of the above: my wife, Angela, and my good friend Dr. Joe Burns.

Knowing God's Love

Introduction

The Ultimate Question

What is God Like?

When you hear the word "God," what is the first thing that comes to mind? For many it is the image of a distant, grumpy —even angry—old man. According to one child, "God is the one who looks around to see who's having fun, so He can stop it!"

Over the last decade I've had the opportunity to put this question to more than a dozen classes of adult Catholics from their mid-twenties to their late seventies, and their answers have included the following:

"He doesn't think about me; God's too busy with more important things than to think about me."

"He's disappointed in me."

"He's frustrated or angry with me because I keep failing in the same ways over and over again."

"He sees me as the failure that I really am."

These aren't the answers of uncatechized, maladjusted, or "problem" adults. They are well-educated, successful, business-people, parish leaders, doctors, and parents (some have sons who are priests and daughters who are in religious life). On average these adults are in their fifth year of an in-depth Catholic Scripture and Catechism program (so rigorous that students can earn undergraduate credits at a nationally renowned university for each year they complete).

But what is God really like? And what does He actually think about us? To answer these questions, we need to begin at the beginning.

Part 1

The Foundational Truths

Truth 1

God Is Love

❖

God is one but not solitary.

—*Catechism of the Catholic Church*, no. 254

Several years ago I heard an interview with the author of the book *All I Really Need to Know I Learned in Kindergarten.* He was humorous and insightful, and his premise was hard to argue with. Ever since, I've toyed with the idea of writing my own version—*All I Really Need to Know I Learned in the First Three Chapters of Genesis.* I mean, it's all there—the answers to humanity's deepest questions: Where did I come from? Why am I here? What is the meaning of life? Who is God? Why did He create me? What is He like?

To answer the fundamental question *What is God like?* we turn to the first chapter of Genesis. We'll start by considering the first thing that God revealed about Himself: "In the beginning God created the heavens and the earth" (Gen. 1:1). This tells us the first thing that God did—He created—but not who He is. To answer that, we need to read a little further: "Then God said, 'Let us make man in our image, after our likeness'" (Gen. 1:26).

Knowing God's Love

God Is a "We"

So, the first thing that God revealed about Himself is that He is a "We," which theologians refer to as *a communion of persons*. Citing one of the earliest Christian creeds,[2] the *Catechism of the Catholic Church* put it this way: "God is one but not solitary."[3] Even though God is one, that one God exists as a "We."

This is so unexpected—and significant—that He repeated it three times in one short sentence: "Let *us* make man in *our* image, after *our* likeness." Consider the implications: Before anything else in all of creation existed, before the universe was made, before the stars gave their first light, before the planets came into being, before galaxies, before the angels, even before the creation of time itself, there existed an eternal "We."

God Is a God of Relationship

Thus, it is not too much to say that the ultimate, foundational truth of the universe—that which precedes all else, and on which everything else is dependent—is relationship. God is a God of relationship. And as we'll see, everything else in all of creation originates from this original truth.

Its importance cannot be overstated. For example, theologians of one of the world's major non-Christian religions believe that, while God can choose to love, it is impossible for Him to *be* love. Love must have an object—someone or something to be loved.[4] "Who," they ask, "did God love before

---

[2] *Fides Damasi*: DS 71, as quoted in CCC 254.

[3] CCC 254.

[4] John Haddad and Douglas Groothuis, "Allah, The Trinity, and Divine Love," *Christian Research Journal* 36, no. 5 (2013), http://www.equip.org/article/allah-the-trinity-and-divine-love/.

He created?" As the only eternal being, He was alone and had no one else to love. Thus love could only be something that He chose to do *after* He created. In the view of such people, God is power and will. The first thing He did was create, exercising His will through His power. And this belief has shaped all of their subsequent teachings regarding marriage, family life, social justice, government, politics, and so forth, with sobering consequences.

Other people go so far as to say that God created because He was lonely and needed someone to keep Him company.[5]

God Is Love

The Christian God is very different from either of these gods, and what He revealed about Himself is indisputably clear—God *is love* (1 John 4:8).

He can *be* love—because He is a "We." He has always existed as a relationship, a communion of persons, and now we see that this communion is a relationship of love. Only a God who is a "We" can also be a God who is love.

The love of God is so real, so substantive, that it is actually a person. In Christian theology we know this God, who is a "We," as the Trinity—the Father, the Son, and the Holy Spirit. And the Holy Spirit *is* the love between the Father and the Son. He is their love "personified," in that the self-giving love between the Father and the Son "proceeds" as the very person of God, the Holy Spirit.

Pope St. John Paul II explained it this way:

---

[5] Sean McDowell, "Did God Create the World Because He Was Lonely?" *Sean McDowell* (blog), October 6, 2015, http://sean mcdowell.org/blog/was-god-ever-lonely.

> The ... Father and the Son are not only united by that mutual love.... Their reciprocal love proceeds in them and from them as a person. The ... Holy Spirit.[6]

Thus, the Nicene Creed states that:

> We believe in one God, the Father ... the Son ... and the Holy Spirit,... who proceeds from the Father and the Son.[7]

So the answer to the question "Whom did God love before He created?" is simple—Himself. The one God has always existed in three distinct Persons, loving each other. And they still do, and always have, and always will—from all eternity. Thus, God is love.

Self-Giving for the Benefit of Another

But what is love? When we say that God is love, what do we mean? Since He is love, it makes sense to go to His teachings for the definition of love. In the Gospel of John He said there is no greater love than to lay down one's life for another (see John 15:13).

Love, then, is self-giving for the benefit of another—to give of oneself, to lay down one's life, for the good of another. St. Paul shared several applications of this when he noted that:

> Love is patient and kind; love is not jealous or boastful; it is not arrogant or rude. Love does not insist on its own

---

[6] Pope St. John Paul II, General Audience, "The Holy Spirit Proceeds from the Father and the Son," November 20, 1985, no. 3.

[7] CCC, sect. 1.

way; it is not irritable or resentful; it does not rejoice at wrong, but rejoices in the right. Love bears all things, believes all things, hopes all things, endures all things. Love never ends. (1 Cor. 13:4–8)

And each of these characteristics of love is applied in the context of relationship; each is a specific way of laying down one's life for the good of another.

❖

Summary: God Is Love

In this book's introduction we asked two fundamental questions: (1) What is God like? and (2) What does He think of us? In this chapter we discovered the surprising answer to the first question:

❖ God is a "We" — a communion of persons — a God of relationship.

❖ God is love — He has always existed as a relationship of love.

❖ His love is so real, so substantive, that it is actually a person — the Holy Spirit.

❖ Our understanding of God as relationship, a communion of persons, shapes our subsequent beliefs regarding marriage, family life, social justice, government, politics, and so forth and has significant consequences for each of these. This will be explored further in later chapters.

❖ Love is self-giving for the benefit of another — to lay down one's life for another.

❖ So, finally, love is lived in the context of relationship — the characteristics of love that St. Paul listed are practical ways to lay down one's life for the good of another.

Knowing God's Love

Now that we know what God is like, in His essence, in the eternal nature of His being, we are closer to answering our second question: What does He think of us?

In order to answer this question, we must first discover what God has said about who *we* are.

Truth 2

Man Is Created in God's Image

❖

*Man becomes the image of God not so much in the
moment of solitude as in the moment of communion.*

—Pope St. John Paul II, General Audience, November 14, 1979

To answer our second question—"What does God think about us?"—we need to return to Genesis to see what He tells us about who we are:

> So God created man in his own image, in the image of God he created him; male and female he created them. (Gen. 1:27)

The first thing we learned about God is that He is a "We," and now the first thing we learn about man is that he is a "they." A specific "they"—male and female, created in God's image.

A Caution Regarding Analogies

Although analogies can help us to understand certain things in the spiritual realm (God Himself used them regularly: "The kingdom of God is like a mustard seed ... a pearl ... a hidden treasure," and so forth), the Church provides us with this important caution:

"With every similarity (between the created order and the Creator), there is always an even greater dissimilarity. Ultimately God is utterly incomparable to anything created."[8] After all, in using analogies, Jesus didn't mean to say that the Kingdom of God is a tiny physical object that you can hold in your hand, or something you could buy at a jewelry store, or an item you could lock in a safe to protect it from thieves. Each of these analogies does tell us something about the kingdom, but none of them tells us everything about it. The same principle holds true regarding the image of God in man that we are about to consider. God is infinitely above our understanding, and although certain aspects of our nature point back to, or reflect, certain aspects of His nature, He remains *utterly incomparable to anything created.*

Man Is a "They"

These words sound so simple and ordinary that it's easy to miss their significance, but if we do, we miss a critical truth about who we are. Just as God exists as an eternal communion of persons (the Trinity), man also exists, "from the beginning" (Matt. 19:8), as a communion of persons — male and female. Thus, when Scripture refers to "man" it speaks of both male and female, just as when it talks about God, it speaks of the Trinity.

As St. Augustine noted, "The Holy Spirit ... is something common to the Father and the Son. But this communion itself is consubstantial and coeternal; and if it may fitly be called friendship, let it be so called; but it is most aptly called love."[9] Thus,

---

[8] *Fourth Lateran Council* (1215), 2, http://www.papalencyclicals. net/Councils/ecum12-2.htm#On the error of abbot Joachim.

[9] St. Augustine, *De trinitate* 6, 5 (7) (PL 42, 928), as cited in David Coffey, "The Holy Spirit as the Mutual Love of the Father and the Son," *Theological Studies* 51 (1990): p. 4.

because God is a "We" whose love is so real that it is actually a person (the Holy Spirit), man—made in God's image—is a "they" whose love is so real that it can also become a person.

The love between a man and a woman is designed to generate life, a new human being—one who has the same nature, value, and dignity as the parents—equal to them, yet distinct and unique. In a mysterious and nonphysical way, this points to the love of the Trinity, in which the Holy Spirit, who is equal to the Father and the Son, proceeds from their love as a unique, distinct person. Of course, language fails us here because the Father and the Son and the Holy Spirit have always existed together, as one single God, from all eternity. There was never a time when the love between the Father and the Son was not the Holy Spirit, and there is no physicality involved whatsoever, so the analogy quickly breaks down if we take it further than Church has. Yet, as we saw from St. John Paul II in the last chapter:

> The ... Father and the Son are not only united by that mutual love.... Their reciprocal love proceeds in them and from them as a person. The ... Holy Spirit.[10]

The First Commandment

Do you know what the first commandment in Scripture is? People usually think of the first and greatest commandment: to love God with all your heart and your neighbor as yourself (see Matt. 22:37, 39). Although we'll consider that commandment later, I'm referring to the first one found written in Scripture: "And God blessed them, saying, 'Be fruitful and multiply and fill ... the earth'" (Gen. 1:28).

---

[10] John Paul II, "The Holy Spirit Proceeds," 3.

Love and Intimacy

So the first command that God gave us is to make love—that's what this commandment means, right? And let's face it: it comes as quite a surprise to many non-Christians (and, sadly, even to some Christians). Maybe that's because of the media's frequent portrayal of Christianity as having a prudish, suppressed, even negative view of human sexuality. Yet nothing could be further from the truth.

God could have chosen any method for the procreation of the human race. He could have made us like amoeba, where one simply divides in two in order to form a new life (science-fiction writers seem particularly intrigued with that option). But He created sexual relations—between a husband and wife—as the means for generating new life because they best image what He wanted us to know about his nature, which is:

+ self-giving love
+ that causes joy
+ and can lead to new life

Joy and Pleasure

In addition to being a God of relationships, He is also a God of joy.[11] Thus, in His image and likeness we are made for joy and to take pleasure in the self-giving love from which new life comes. That is why the Catechism says:

> The acts in marriage by which the intimate ... union of the spouses takes place ... are noble and honorable; the truly human performance of these acts fosters the

---

[11] Ps. 37:4; Matt. 25:21, 23; Luke 15; John 15:11; 17:13; Rom. 14:17; 15:13; Phil. 3:1; 4:4.

self-giving they signify and enriches the spouses in joy and gratitude. Sexuality is a source of joy and pleasure.

The Creator himself ... established that in the [generative] function, spouses should experience pleasure and enjoyment of body and spirit. (CCC 2362)

Hardwired into the Universe

God so wanted us to understand the importance of relationships—as the foundation of his nature and, thus, of all reality—that He hardwired signs of it throughout creation.

St. Paul put it this way:

What can be known about God is plain ... because God has shown it.... Ever since the creation of the world his invisible nature ... has been clearly perceived in the things that have been made. (Rom. 1:19–20)

And the psalmist noted that:

The heavens declare the glory of God, and the sky above proclaims his handiwork. (Ps. 19:1, ESV)

Dice in Space

Although it's easier to see these signs in the animal world, even the behavior of inanimate objects can point to relationship's significance. Do you know what would happen if you took a pair of dice into outer space, placed them several inches apart, and left them there, motionless?

According to a scientist on the Discovery Channel (2011), over time they would gradually come together. Because of gravity they would be drawn together until they "merged," until they touched each other in space; until they came into a physical "relationship" with each other. Thus even inanimate objects gravitate toward "relationship."[12]

The First "Not Good"

Now, let's return to Genesis. In the creation account the most frequent thing that God said is that it was good or very good (see Gen. 1:4–31). He said it six times in just one chapter. This leads to the question: What was the first "not good"?

Before studying John Paul II's Theology of the Body, I thought that the first "not good" was the Fall—man's first sin. Because God, who is perfect, created everything, how could anything have been "not good" before sin? You can imagine my surprise when I learned what the first "not good" actually was: "It is not good that the man should be alone" (Gen. 2:18).

God said this before the Fall, before our descent into sin. Knowing that God is a "We" and that in His image we are created to be a "they," it is clear why it would not be good for the man to be alone. Alone, Adam was not a "they"; he did not exist as a communion of persons[13] in the way that God does, so he did not reflect that aspect of God's image.

Naming the Animals

But it is surprising to see what God did next. Immediately after saying it was not good for the man to be alone, He brought "every beast of the field and every bird of the air ... to the man to see what he would call them: (Gen. 2:19). God asked Adam to

---

[12] Ron Kurtus, "Gravitational Force between Two Objects," Ron Kurtus' School for Champions, revised February 2016, http://www.school-for-champions.com/science/gravitation_force_objects.htm#.V17vBfkrLIU.

[13] Bl. Pope Paul VI, *Gaudium et spes*, 12.

name the animals. But why ask him to do that? The narrative continues: "The man gave names to all cattle, and to the birds of the air, and to every beast of the field; but for the man there was not found a helper fit for him" (Gen. 2:20).

God wanted to make it clear that, in Adam's role as the image and likeness of God, nothing he had yet created was a "helper fit" for Adam. But a helper fit for Adam to do what?

To help him reflect the image and likeness of God as communion of persons. For that, Adam needed someone like himself, someone with whom he could also become a "we." As John Paul II put it:

> Alone, man does not completely realize this essence.... He realizes it only by existing "with someone" — and even more deeply and completely — by existing "for someone."[14] Man becomes the image of God not so much in the moment of solitude as in the moment of communion.[15]

Bone of My Bone

So, for us to reflect fully the image of God—who exists as relationship of love between equals—we also need an equal "someone" to love: a someone who has the same nature as we do yet is distinct from us—a someone about whom Adam could say, "This at last is bone of my bones and flesh of my flesh" (Gen. 2:23).

The religions that believe that God had to create because He was lonely may be onto something. They had the right concept

---

[14] John Paul II, *Man and Woman He Created Them, A Theology of the Body*, translated by Michael Waldstein (Boston: Pauline Books and Media, 2006), p. 182.

[15] Ibid., p. 163.

but the wrong application. We are the ones who needed God to create—not so that He wouldn't be lonely, but so that we could live in His image.

Adam, the male, needed God to complete his creation with Eve, the female. Adam and Eve needed each other in order to become a "they," in order to form a new "them" in God's image. It is in this spousal relationship that we are first called to give ourselves generously, for the benefit of the other, and thus to image God's love as a communion of persons.

Satan's Envy

Christianity teaches that Satan fell because of pride.[16] And St. Thomas further notes that Satan's fall included the sin of envy:

> After the sin of pride, there followed the evil of envy in the sinning angel, whereby he grieved over man's good [as] ... God makes use of man for the Divine glory.[17]

And the Catechism adds:

> Behind the disobedient choice of our first parents lurks a seductive voice, opposed to God, which makes them fall into death out of envy.[18]

The book of Wisdom further clarifies:

> God created man for incorruption, and made him in the image of his own eternity, but through the devil's envy death entered the world (Wisd. 2:23–24).

---

[16] St. Thomas Aquinas, *Summa Theologica*, I, Q. 63, art. 2.
[17] Ibid.
[18] CCC 397.

I always found this hard to understand. What could Satan possibly envy in man? According to Scripture he was "the signet of perfection, full of wisdom and perfect in beauty" (Ezek. 28:12), he was the shrewdest, most astute of all God's creatures (Gen. 3:1), he was an "anointed guardian cherub ... on the holy mountain of God" (Ezek. 28:15), and even now he "disguises himself as an angel of light" (2 Cor. 11:14). What could he possibly envy in us?

Procreation, Co-Creation, Speculation

St. Thomas Aquinas, known as the Angelic Doctor in part because of his expertise in angels,[19] offers us a surprising hint to the question of what Satan could envy in us. After first noting many of the ways that angels are superior to men, Thomas goes on to say:

> We may consider the image of God in man as regards its accidental qualities, so far as to observe in man a certain imitation of God, consisting in the fact that man proceeds from man, as God from God.... In these and like things the image of God is more perfect in man than it is in the angels ... [although] we must grant that, absolutely speaking, the angels are more to the image of God than man is, but that in some respects man is more like to God.[20]

Angels do not—in fact, they cannot—fulfill the very first commandment of God. They are not able to "be fruitful and

---

[19] "Why We Call Him the 'Angelic Doctor,'" The New Theological Movement, posted January 28, 2013, by Fr. Ryan Erlenbush, http://newtheologicalmovement.blogspot.com/2013/01/why-we-call-him-angelic-doctor.html.

[20] St. Thomas Aquinas, Summa Theologica, I, Q. 93, art. 3.

multiply." They do not procreate.[21] Instead, the book of Hebrews notes that angels are "ministering spirits sent forth to serve, for the sake of those who are to obtain salvation" (Heb. 1:14).

Thus, at least part of what Satan envies in man may be our ability to reflect the image of God (who is love itself) through our marital relations. I don't mean to imply that there is something about the physical act of conjugal relations itself that Satan, as a pure spiritual being, envies, but that he might be jealous of our ability to cooperate with God in bringing into existence new creatures who are made in the image of God—and who will bring Him glory for all eternity.

Satan's pride seems to have made it intolerable that, as a perfect, pure spiritual being, his role was to serve, for our sake, in order that we might obtain salvation. And to make matters worse, we were given the supreme honor of being the only creatures in all of creation who can cooperate in bringing new persons into being: persons who are also created in God's image. This appears to have been more than the evil one was willing to accept.

This Explains a Lot

All of this helps to explain why the forbidden fruit in the Garden of Eden is often misrepresented as having something to do with sex:

> One … view is that the forbidden fruit is not a fruit at all, but a metaphorical one, possibly the fruit of the womb, i.e. sex and procreation.[22]

---

[21] See Matt. 22:30.

[22] "Forbidden Fruit: Identifying the Fruit," American Pink, http://america.pink/forbidden-fruit_1580612.html.

Man Is Created in God's Image

It also helps explain why so much in life seems to revolve around sex—as well as why so much that is related to sex seems to be in such a desperately broken and unsatisfactory state. The answers become clear when we consider what happened immediately after Adam and Eve sinned:

> [S]he took of its fruit and ate; and she also gave some to her husband, and he ate. Then the eyes of both were opened, and they knew that they were naked; and they sewed fig leaves together and made themselves aprons. (Gen. 3:6–7)

The first thing they realized was that they were naked, and the shame of that led them to hide their specific maleness and femaleness from each other. Something had gone wrong in their very core—in their ability to be male and female as a gift for each other, in their sexuality.

The initial result of the Fall, then, was a corruption of their sexual nature—a corruption in that very part of their being that made them most able to image the likeness of God, as John Paul II explained:

> Man becomes the image of God not so much in the moment of solitude as in the moment of communion.[23]

This corruption meant that they could no longer see their bodies as they were created to be, a sign of God for each other:

> The human body bore in itself, in the mystery of creation, an unquestionable sign of the "image of God."[24]

---

[23] John Paul II, *Man and Woman*, p. 163.
[24] Ibid., p. 241.

The human body, with its sex—masculinity and femininity—includes "from the beginning" ... the power to express love, precisely that love in which the human person becomes a gift and—through this gift—fulfills the very meaning of his being and existence.[25]

Now, rather than experiencing their bodies as gifts to be given to each other, as an expression of God's love, they felt the impulse to hide their bodies from each other.

This was the opposite of what God had intended:

That original nakedness, mutual and at the same time not weighed down by shame, expresses this interior freedom of man.... At the root of their nakedness is the interior freedom of the gift—the disinterested gift of oneself.[26]

The freedom of the gift is the response to the deep awareness of the gift.... Through this truth and freedom love is built up, which we must affirm is authentic love.[27]

Thus, their ability to love freely, authentically, and disinterestedly (not looking to what they could receive, but to what they could give), was severely damaged.

The First Thing to Go

Only in the light of these truths does the full significance of St. Paul's teaching regarding the effects of sin become clear:

They became vain in their reasoning, and their senseless minds were darkened. While claiming to be wise, they

[25] Ibid., pp. 185–186.
[26] Ibid., pp. 184, 187.
[27] John Paul II, General Audience, May 30, 1984, 5.

became fools … and [were handed] over to impurity through the lusts of their hearts for the mutual degradation of their bodies. They exchanged the truth of God for a lie and [were handed] over to degrading passions. Their females exchanged natural relations for unnatural, and the males likewise gave up natural relations with females and burned with lust for one another. (Rom. 1:21–27, NABRE)

A result of sin, then, which damages our relationship with God, is the corruption of our ability to *image* God through our sexual nature. This is why the *Catechism*, in speaking of the Fall, says:

The harmony in which they had found themselves … is now destroyed: the control of the soul's spiritual faculties over the body is shattered; the union of man and woman becomes subject to tensions, their relations henceforth marked by lust and domination (CCC 400).

Lust is the corruption of that co-creative desire within marriage that can lead to new life. Domination is the corruption of our ability to make a sincere "gift of self" that can lead to the co-creative, marital act. Thus, at the deepest level, sin has corrupted our ability to live out our authentic masculinity and femininity.

The Real Apple

As we've seen, the first sin had nothing to do with sex. Sex is a gift from God. Through such a gift, spouses are meant to be the image of God's love to each other, by being a gift to each other, in a way that can generate new life. It is a great good given by God, "who richly provides us with all things for our enjoyment" (1 Tim. 6:17, NABRE). This is why we are cautioned not to be deceived but to recognize that God is the giver of "every good and perfect gift that comes from above" (cf. James 16–17). Nonetheless, sin's tragic consequences have seriously harmed our ability to live as gifts to one another, in our maleness and femaleness.

Original sin, and all subsequent sin, has the same root. What Eve did when she listened to Satan and ate the fruit, what Adam did when he accepted the fruit from her as a counterfeit "gift," and what you and I do every time we choose sin, is all the same. As one of the most poignant passages in the *Catechism* notes:

> Man, tempted by the devil, let his trust in his Creator die in his heart and, abusing his freedom, disobeyed God's command. This is what man's first sin consisted of. All subsequent sin would be disobedience toward God and lack of trust in his goodness. (CCC 397)

Sin, then, is disobeying God because, in our hearts, we choose not to trust in God's goodness toward us—not to believe in His love for us.

❖

Summary: Man Is Created in God's Image

In the first chapter, we answered the question "What is God like?" and found that:

✢ God is a "We"—a communion of persons, a God of relationship.

✢ He is love—God exists as relationship of love.

✢ God's love is so real that it is actually a person, the Holy Spirit.

✢ And that love is self-giving for the benefit of another.

Man Is Created in God's Image

In this chapter we sought to find what God has revealed about us—about who and what we are—and we learned that:

+ Man is a "they"—made in God's image—meant to live in a communion of persons.
+ Man is a specific "they"—male and female.
+ In God's image, we are also made to exist in relationship. Thus, we can realize our true nature only by existing *with someone*—and even more deeply and completely—by existing *for someone.*
+ Creation itself is hardwired to remind us of the foundational importance of relationship; even inanimate objects can remind us of this truth.
+ Sex was not the cause of the Fall. It is a great good, a gift from God, which is meant to be enjoyed in gratitude by the spouses.
+ Marriage, as a sign of God's love, is designed to lead to new life through procreation.
+ Original sin, and all subsequent sin, is ultimately the result of a pride that fails to trust in God's goodness toward us.

In the next chapter, we'll consider the implications of these truths as we look to answer the question "What does God think about us?"

Truth 3

God Desires Us

❖

All I want is an intimate friendship with you. . . .
You are everything to me, brother, co-heir, friend,
and associate. What more do you want?

—Jesus, as paraphrased by St. John
Chrysostom, *Homilies on St. Matthew*, 76

In the prologue of the *Catechism* we find this heartening explanation as to why God created man in the first place:

> God, infinitely perfect and blessed in himself, in a plan
> of sheer goodness, freely created man to make him share
> in his own blessed life. (CCC 1)

God had no need to create us because He was already infinitely perfect. And He was already blessed in Himself, which means that He was completely happy.[28] We could add nothing to His perfection or happiness. Instead, we see that, "in a plan

---

[28] *Strong's Concordance*, 3107, "makarios," short definition: happy, blessed, http://biblehub.com/greek/3107.htm.

of sheer goodness, he freely created man to … share in his own blessed life."

So the reason God created us was so that we could share in His infinite love and thus experience His perfect joy and happiness. That is why we are told that "man is the only creature on earth that God willed for itself."[29]

God created us for *us*. His love is so abundant, so joyful, and so real that He wanted to share it—so He created man, as the crown of His creation. He gave us His image and likeness in a way that nothing else in all of creation has—in our ability to participate in co-creating others who are also made in that image; others who can then share in that co-creative process of love themselves.

As we saw in chapter 2, our response to this indescribable gift was to reject God's love.

The God of the Clipboard

Have you ever had the sneaking suspicion that someone is watching you? That sense that someone is keeping track of your every move, taking notes on what you are doing? No, I'm not talking about the scandals involving the NSA or the IRS.

Deep down, at the level of our underlying assumptions (those things that we believe and that we take for granted, but that we rarely examine or say out loud), don't we feel that God may be more like a hall monitor than anything else? That He wanders the halls of our lives with a clipboard, watching in order to catch us doing something wrong so that He can write it in our "permanent record" and mete out the appropriate punishment? That may have been how Adam and Eve felt, since their first

---

[29] Paul VI, *Gaudium et spes*, 24.

reaction when they did something wrong was to hide from God (see Gen. 3:10).

Surely, we think, a perfect God of love who created us only for our own good, to share in His joy and happiness, to share in the ongoing work of creation, a God who even richly gave us all things to enjoy, would want nothing to do with us after we so heartlessly rejected Him.

And in our own lives, in our hearts where no one else sees, we know all too well the truth that *we all, like sheep, have gone astray*, "each of us has turned to his own way" (Isa. 53:6, NIV) and that "none is righteous" (Rom. 3:10).

In our more reflective moments, don't we have to admit with St. Paul that, very often, "I do not do the good I want, but the evil I do not want is what I do.... [W]hen I want to do right, evil is close at hand" (Rom. 7:19, 21). We understand from our own experience why, when Jesus said, "Let him who is without sin among you be the first to throw a stone" they all went away, one by one (John 8:7, 9).

The God of the Prodigal

Yet God did not turn away from us when we turned away from Him. In fact, He did the opposite. When Jesus wanted to show what God thinks of us, He took a story that was familiar to His audience and gave it a remarkably different ending.

You'll remember the story from Luke 15. A son went to his father and asked for his inheritance. In effect, he said that he wished his father were already dead, because an inheritance is only distributed after someone dies. Surprisingly, the father agreed to this cold-hearted request and gave him the inheritance.

"Not many days later" the son took his inheritance and "took his journey into a far country." In moving far away, he reiterated that he wanted nothing to do with his father. He then "squandered [the inheritance] in loose living" (Luke 15:13).

Later, when the son was starving and destitute, he came to himself and decided to return home. He resolved to apologize, to ask for his father's forgiveness, and to seek a job as his hired servant, recognizing that he was "no longer worthy to be called [his] son" (Luke 15:19).

Stories like this were fairly common in first-century Palestine. They were a type of morality tale used to teach children important cultural lessons, and everyone knew the correct ending to this particular story. The father would have turned the son away, cast him out, and might even have refused to speak to him. If he did speak, it would have been to say something like, "Depart from me. I don't know you—I no longer have a son. The son I once had is now dead to me." And the community would have performed a *kezazah* ceremony on the son: "They would break a large pot in front of him and yell, 'You are now cut off from your people!' The community would totally reject him."[30]

So what happened in Jesus' version would have been a complete shock to his audience. Jesus said that, while the son was still far off, "his father saw him and had compassion, and ran and embraced him and kissed him" (Luke 15:20). To appreciate fully the impact that this would have had on His listeners, there is something else we need to know about their culture:

In the first century ... a Middle Eastern man never—never—ran. If he were to run, he would have to hitch up his tunic so he would not trip. If he did this, it would

<hr>

[30] Matt Williams, "The Prodigal Son's Father Shouldn't Have Run!", *Biola Magazine* (Summer 2010), http://magazine.biola.edu/.

show his bare legs. In that culture, it was humiliating and shameful for a man to show his bare legs.[31]

So why did the father run? "In order to get to his son before he entered the village ... before the community gets to him, so that his son does not experience the shame and humiliation of their taunting and rejection."[32]

Thus, instead of rejecting his son, the father chose to protect him while he was still at a distance. The father humiliated himself—both in accepting his son back and in running out to meet him—in order to protect him from the humiliation and shame of the *kezazah* ceremony.

To indicate further "how great a love the father has lavished upon us" (1 John 3:1, NIV), Jesus continued:

And the son said to him, "Father, I have sinned against heaven and before you; I am no longer worthy to be called your son." But the father said to his servants, "Bring quickly the best robe, and put it on him; and put a ring on his hand, and shoes on his feet; and bring the fatted calf and kill it, and let us eat and make merry; for this my son was dead, and is alive again; he was lost, and is found." And they began to make merry. (Luke 15:21–24)

Thus, the father not only restored the son to his former place of honor (signified by the robe) and authority (signified by the ring), but he also hosted an extravagant celebration to mark his return!

---

[31] Ibid.
[32] Ibid.

And that is how God looks at you and me. He eagerly awaits our return and desires to make us His children again, to welcome us with open arms, and to hold a celebration for us when we return—a celebration so big that even the angels rejoice when just one of us repents (Luke 15:10), when one of us returns home to our heavenly father.

Father of Mercy

So it turns out that God really is watching over us—just as we suspected, He is following our every move—but for a reason completely different from the one we feared (and without the clipboard). He is looking for a sign of our return, so that, just as in the story of the prodigal, he can run out to greet us: "For God did not send his Son into the world to condemn the world, but to save the world" (John 3:17, NIV). And "the Son of man came to seek and to save the lost" (Luke 19:10), because God is "the Father of mercies and the God of all comfort" (2 Cor. 1:3).

He knows the heights from which we have fallen (see Rev. 2:5) and, incredibly, desires only to bring us back—to restore us to our previous place of joy, honor, and dignity as his children. The entire Bible, from Genesis 3 on, is the story of God seeing us still afar off and running out to meet us. Through both the Old and the New Testaments we see God reaching out to us again and again. In the course of seeking us, He reminds us that He "takes delight in his people" (Ps. 149:4, NIV) and "is moved with compassion because [they] are like sheep without a shepherd" (Matt. 9:36, World English Bible).

He tells us that he "takes pleasure in those who ... hope in his steadfast love" (Ps. 147:11), and He further assures us: "I know the plans I have for you ... plans to prosper you and not to harm you, plans to give you hope and a future" (Jer. 29:11,

NIV) because He "is not willing that any should perish but that all should come to repentance" (2 Pet. 3:9, KJV) and "desires all men to be saved" (1 Tim. 2:4).

As the prologue to the *Catechism of the Catholic Church* puts it:

> For this reason, at every time and in every place, God draws close to man. He calls man to seek him, to know him, to love him with all his strength. He calls together all men, scattered and divided by sin, into the unity of his family, the Church. To accomplish this, when the fullness of time had come, God sent his Son as Redeemer and Savior. In his Son and through him, he invites men to become, in the Holy Spirit, his adopted children and thus heirs of his blessed life. (CCC 1)

Mercy and Compassion

It turns out that the God whom we have rejected still loves us deeply:

> As I live, says the Lord GOD, I have no pleasure in the death of the wicked, but that the wicked turn from his way and live. (Ezek. 33:11)

> For the LORD your God is gracious and merciful and will not turn away his face from you, if you return to him. (2 Chron. 30:9)

God's predominant disposition toward us is one of compassion:

> For the mountains may depart and the hills be removed, but my steadfast love shall not depart from you, and my covenant of peace shall not be removed, says the LORD, who has compassion on you. (Isa. 54:10, ESV)

You'll recall that Jesus told His disciples that "whoever has seen me has seen the Father" (John 14:9, ESV). But what did they see in Him? What is it that caused so many sinners to be drawn to Him?[33] The gospel writers tell us that they saw compassion:

> Jesus called his disciples to him and said, "I have compassion on the crowd ... and I am unwilling to send them away." (Matt. 15:32; cf. Mark 8:2)

> And when the Lord saw her, he had compassion on her and said to her, "Do not weep." (Luke 7:13)

In light of our rebellion, the love that God has for us is astonishing. It should cause us to respond with the same joy and awe as St. Paul:

> The Son of God ... loved me and gave himself up for me. (Gal. 2:20)

> What, then, shall we say in response to these things? If God is for us, who can be against us? He who did not spare his own Son, but gave him up for us all—how will he not also, along with him, graciously give us all things? Who will bring any charge against those whom God has chosen? It is God who justifies. Who then is the one who condemns? No one. Christ Jesus who died—more than that, who was raised to life—is at the right hand of God interceding for us. Who shall separate us from the love of Christ? (Rom. 8:31–35, NIV)

---

[33] Matt. 9:11; Mark 2:16; Luke 5:30.

God Desires Us

Good News!

This truth—that God's response to our rebellion has been one of love, mercy, and compassion—is how the gospel got its name. The word "gospel" means "good news" and was used for a message that *brought joy*.[34] It is so prominent a part of the Christian message that the two Greek words that refer to it (the noun *euangelion*, "good news," and the verb *euangelizo*, "to bring or announce good news") occur 130 times in the New Testament![35]

Friends of God

God's love for us is so great that He wants to be our friend, to have a personal, intimate relationship with us, so much so that as Jesus was preparing to undergo His Passion and death, one of the last things He told the apostles was that He had chosen them to be His friends (see John 15:15). He said this to the same apostles who He knew were about to deny and abandon Him in the hour of His greatest need.[36] Even as Judas led the soldiers into the garden to betray Him (echoes of both the Garden of Eden and the story of the prodigal son), Jesus continued to call him His friend (Matt. 26:50).

In the Vatican II document on the Church's missionary activity, *Ad Gentes*, Paul VI reminded us that "God ... calls us to enter into a personal relationship with Him in Christ."[37] Later, John Paul II explained:

---

[34] "What Does the Term 'Gospel' Mean?", Bible.org., https://bible.org/.

[35] Ibid.

[36] "Then all the disciples deserted him and fled" (Matt. 26:56). Peter denies him three times (Matt. 26:69–75).

[37] Paul VI, *Ad Gentes*, 13.

Sometimes even Catholics have lost or never had the chance to experience Christ personally; not Christ as a mere "paradigm" or "value," but as the living Lord, "the way, the truth and the life" (Jn 14:6).[38]

Later, the Holy Father would assert, "Therefore, it is necessary to awaken again in believers a full relationship with Christ."[39] He further advised that "prayer develops that conversation with Christ which makes us his intimate friends: 'Abide in me and I in you' (Jn 15:4)."[40]

An Intimate Friendship

This is the constant teaching of the Catholic Church. St. John Chrysostom, writing around A.D. 390, paraphrased Christ this way: "I am everything, and all I want is an intimate friendship with you.... You are everything to me, brother, co-heir, friend and associate. What more do you want?"[41]

Like their predecessors, more recent popes have continued to emphasize this unchanging teaching:

Pope Paul VI: "[In] conversion ... man [must] realize that he has been snatched away from sin and led into the mystery of God's love, who called him to enter into a personal relationship with Him in Christ.[42]

---

[38] John Paul II, L'Osservatore Romano, March 24, 1993, p. 3.

[39] John Paul II, Ad Limina visit of Bishops of Southern Germany, December 4, 1992.

[40] John Paul II, Novo Millennio Ineunte, 32–33.

[41] St. John Chrysostom, Homilies on St. Matthew, 76.

[42] Paul VI, Ad Gentes, 13.

Pope John Paul II: As you well know it is not a matter of merely passing on a doctrine, but rather of a personal and profound meeting with the Savior.[43]

Pope Benedict XVI: Being Christian is not the result of an ethical choice or a lofty idea, but the encounter with ... a person ... an encounter with the living God.[44]

Everything depends upon an intimate friendship with Jesus.[45]

So the most urgent priority ... is to ... foster the growth of a personal relationship with him.[46]

Pope Francis: God created us in order that we might live in a relationship of deep friendship with him, and even when sin had broken this relationship with God, with others and with creation, God did not abandon us.[47]

As Fr. Dimitri Sala, a Franciscan Friar, put it:

In contemporary language, then, the Christian religion is meant to be practiced in the context of a relationship

[43] John Paul II, "Commissioning of Families of the Neo-Catechumenal Way," *L'Osservatore Romano*, January 14, 1991, p. 12, quoted in Avery Dulles, S.J., John Paul II and the New Evangelization," *America*, February 1, 1992.

[44] Benedict XVI, *Deus Caritas Est*, 1, 28.

[45] Benedict XVI, *Jesus of Nazareth*, vol. I (New York: Doubleday, 2007), p. xii.

[46] Ibid., p. xxiv.

[47] David Uebbing, "Pope: Jesus' Plan for Humanity Requires Catholic Church," *Catholic News Agency*, May 29, 2013, http://www.catholicnewsagency.com/.

with God. Without a personal relationship, our religion is empty — and dead.[48]

The Main Thing

Stephen Covey, author of *The 7 Habits of Highly Effective People*, proposed that, in order to live productive, meaningful lives, we need to ensure one thing. He said we must first identify the one thing that is most important, and then organize our activities around it. As he put it, famously, "The main thing is to keep the main thing the main thing!"[49]

So, if it is true that everything depends on an intimate friendship with Jesus,[50] we would expect to find this idea flowing through all of the Church's teachings. But what do we find? What does the Church say about the "main thing" in regard to her activities?

Evangelization — Invitation to Personal Relationship with God

The first thing we find is that evangelization is meant to be an invitation to a personal relationship with God. John Paul II stated it this way: "Only from a personal relationship with Jesus can an effective evangelization develop."[51]

And Cardinal Ratzinger, as Prefect of the Congregation for the Doctrine of the Faith, said this:

---

[48] Fr. Dimitri Sala, *The Stained Glass Curtain* (Lake Mary, FL: Creation House, 2010), p. 39.

[49] Kevin Kruse, "Stephen Covey: 10 Quotes That Can Change Your Life," *Forbes*, July 16, 2012, http://www.forbes.com/.

[50] Benedict XVI, *Jesus of Nazareth*, vol. I, p. xii.

[51] John Paul II, speech to bishops of Southern Germany, December 4, 1992, *L'Osservatore Romano*, December 23/30, 1992, pp. 5–6.

Evangelization is ... initiation into communion with Jesus ... to evangelize means to acquaint men with Jesus ... to introduce men into a communion of life with him.[52]

The Son of God loved me and gave himself up for me.... We are not an indistinct mass before God. Christ does not and did not treat us as such. In all truth, Christ walked his path for me.... He loved and loves me still. When we have learned to believe this ... to announce it to others as the ... truth, evangelization takes place.[53]

Catechesis—Growing in Intimacy with God

Next we find that in all the Church's varied works of catechesis, the goal is always to help people grow in their intimacy with God. In his apostolic exhortation on catechesis, John Paul II noted:

At the heart of catechesis we find ... a Person, the Person of Jesus of Nazareth.... The definitive aim of catechesis is to put people not only in touch but in communion, in intimacy, with Jesus Christ: only He can lead us to the love of the Father in the Spirit and make us share in the life of the Holy Trinity.[54]

Apostolate—All Activity Directed toward This Relationship

Perhaps most significantly, when defining the Apostolate of the Laity in the Vatican II document *Apostolicam actuositatem*, Paul VI said:

---

[52] Joseph Cardinal Ratzinger, *Gospel, Catechesis, Catechism* (San Francisco: Ignatius Press, 1997), p. 53.

[53] Ibid., p. 71.

[54] John Paul II, *Catechesi tradendae*, 5.

The Church was founded that ... the whole world might enter into a relationship with Christ. All activity ... directed to the attainment of this goal is called the apostolate.... The Christian vocation by its very nature is also a vocation to the apostolate.[55]

Or, to put it more succinctly, Vatican II's seminal document on the laity made it clear that every Christian's vocation is to help people come into a relationship with Jesus Christ. All of this supports our conclusion that a personal relationship with God is "the main thing" of the Catholic Church.

Simple, Profound, Radiant

On September 19, 2013, Pope Francis reminded us that the gospel *attracts*, *fascinates*, and *makes the heart burn* when we "focus on the essentials," so he called on all Christians to "proclaim the Gospel in a way that is more simple, profound, and radiant."[56]

What could be more simple, profound, and radiant than the knowledge that, despite our sin, God still desires an intimate friendship with us and that He invites us to become His "dearly loved children" (Eph. 5:1, NIV)?

What Is Conversion?

Now that we know what God thinks of us—that He sees us as His dearly loved children and He wants an intimate friendship with us—what's next? What do we need to do?

[55] Paul VI, *Apostolicam actuositatem*, 2.
[56] "Proclaim Fullness of Gospel, Pope Teaches in Interview," Catholic News Agency, September 19, 2013, http://www.catholicnews agency.com/.

Like the prodigal, we must repent. To repent means to change our mind and to think differently, particularly with reference to God and to His will.[57] In other words, we need to reverse the decision that Adam and Eve made in the Garden. Instead of giving in to the temptation to "let trust in [our] Creator die in [our] hearts," we need to choose to "trust in his goodness" toward us (see CCC 397). In a spirit of humility, we need to admit that our previous thoughts about God were wrong and choose to believe in Him, as He is—the God of relationship, who is Love itself.

This is the first step, and each of us needs to take it for ourselves. Although it can seem daunting, God has already given us the ability to take it. This is the initial conversion that Paul VI was referring to when he said:

> This conversion must be taken as ... initial ... yet sufficient to make a man realize that he has been snatched away from sin and led into the mystery of God's love, who called him to enter into a personal relationship with Him in Christ.[58]

Or, as the Acts of the Apostles recounts:

> Now when they heard this they were cut to the heart, and said to Peter and the rest of the apostles, "Brethren, what shall we do?" And Peter said to them, "Repent, and be baptized every one of you in the name of Jesus Christ for the forgiveness of your sins; and you shall receive the gift of the Holy Spirit. For the promise is to you and to your children and to all that are far off." (Acts 2:37–39)

---

[57] *Strong's Concordance*, 3340, "metanoeó," http://biblehub.com/greek/3340.htm.

[58] Paul VI, *Ad Gentes*, 13.

As John Paul II put it: "Conversion means accepting, by a personal decision, the saving sovereignty of Christ and becoming his disciple."[59]

An Invitation to Relationship

If you've never made that personal decision before, that decision to trust in God's goodness toward you and to accept the forgiveness and salvation He offers, why not take a moment to do so now? Like the prodigal, tell Him that you are sorry for not trusting Him before and that you also want to return home. You can become His child, and a disciple (follower) of His Son Jesus.

❖

Summary: God Desires Us

❖ In a plan of sheer goodness, God freely created man to share in His own blessed life — He created us for us. As Paul VI put it, man is the only creature on earth that God willed for itself.

❖ The God of relationship created us for relationship with Him so we could participate in the perfect life of the Trinity.

❖ Through sin, we broke that relationship.

❖ Yet, God's predominant disposition toward us is not anger, but love, mercy, and compassion.

❖ God actually delights in the sons of men (see Prov. 8:31, NASB).

---

[59] John Paul II, *Redemptoris Missio*, 46.

God Desires Us

+ The entire Bible, from Genesis 3 on, is the story of God calling us back into relationship with Him. His desire is to have a personal, intimate friendship with us.
+ Jesus came not to condemn us but to save us.
+ As Benedict XVI put it, "Everything depends upon an intimate friendship with Jesus, so the most urgent priority is to foster the growth of a personal relationship with him."
+ This is "the main thing" of the Catholic Church. Thus, Evangelization, conversion, catechesis, and the apostolate are all directed toward this goal.
+ Finally, God calls each one of us, individually, to repentance and invites us to accept his forgiveness
+ To repent is to change our mind about God and to reverse the decision that Adam and Eve made in the Garden.
+ Instead of giving in to the temptation to let trust in our Creator die in our hearts, we need to choose to trust in His goodness toward us. In doing so, we become disciples of Jesus—His followers.

Part 2

The Foundational Truths
Applied Personally

Truth 4

To Work Is to Share in God's Creation

❖

The knowledge that by means of work man shares in the work of
creation constitutes the most profound motive for undertaking it.

—Pope St. John Paul II, *Laborem exercens*, 25

We began by looking at the first thing God revealed about
Himself: that He is a "We," a God of relationship. Then
we learned that man is a "they," male and female—created for
and from relationship. Now let's look at the first thing that God
did:

> In the beginning God created the heavens and the
> earth.... And God saw everything that he had made,
> and behold, it was very good.... Thus the heavens and
> the earth were finished.... And on the seventh day God
> finished his work which he had done, and he rested on
> the seventh day from all his work. (Gen. 1:1, 31; 2:1–2)

In this passage we see that the first thing God did in the Bible account was work—He created the heavens and the earth,
He saw everything He had made, He finished His work, and He
rested from His work. The words used to describe His work include

"created," "made," "separated," "gathered," and "set" (as in to set something in place). Fifteen times we are told that God performed some type of work. So, in addition to being a God of relationship, He is also a God of work.

But for whom did God work? Who was the beneficiary of all this creating, making, gathering and setting? Let's return to the prologue of the *Catechism of the Catholic Church*:

> God, infinitely perfect and blessed in himself, in a plan
> of sheer goodness freely created man to make him share
> in his own blessed life.

God worked out of sheer goodness — for our benefit. This makes sense because He is love, and as we saw, love is self-giving for the benefit of another. So He worked not for His own benefit but for ours — and He continues to do so.[60]

Work in the Image of God

Since we are created in God's image, what are the implications — for us — of his being a God of work? The first command He gave us, to be fruitful and multiply, paralleled the first truth we learned about Him — that He is a "We." Now we discover that the next command He gave us parallels the first thing He did — He worked:

> And God blessed them, and God said to them, "Be fruitful
> and multiply, and fill the earth and subdue it." ... The
> LORD God took the man and put him in the Garden of
> Eden to till it and keep it. (Gen. 1:28; 2:15)

---

[60] "My Father is working still, and I am working" (John 5:17).

This subduing, tilling, and keeping was physical work. Thus, man was given two tasks to do in imaging God:

✢ Be fruitful and multiply (make love and have children).
✢ Make the earth fruitful, and care for it (subdue, till, and keep it).

Intellectual and Physical Work

God also gave man intellectual work to do:

> Out of the ground the LORD God formed every beast of the field and every bird of the air, and brought them to the man to see what he would call them; and whatever the man called every living creature, that was its name. The man gave names to all cattle, and to the birds of the air, and to every beast of the field. (Gen. 2:19–20)

So caring for the earth and making it fruitful consisted of two types of work:

✢ physical—subduing, tilling, and keeping
✢ intellectual—naming the animals

Thus physical and intellectual work have equal dignity because they are both ordained by God, and are each part of the way that we are designed to *image* Him. John Paul II noted:

> In carrying out this mandate ... every human being, reflects the very action of the Creator of the Universe ... and so these words, placed at the very beginning of the Bible, never cease to be relevant.[61]

It is important to remember that the command to work was given *before* the Fall, not after it. It was not given as a punishment

---

[61] John Paul II, *Laborem exercens*, 4.

for sin, but as a gift to enable us to live in God's image—to share completely in His own blessed, happy life.

Work as a Duty

John Paul II went on to say:

> Work is an obligation ... a duty, on the part of man.... Man must work, both because the Creator has commanded it and because of his own humanity, which requires work in order to be maintained and developed.[62]

Therefore, because we are created in God's image, we must work, even as He did and does. It is fundamental to who we are. Not to work would be not to live in that image.

As St. Irenaeus said, "The glory of God is man fully alive,"[63] and to be fully alive we must work. Moreover, our work should benefit others, as God's work does:

> Man must work out of regard for others, especially his own family, but also for the society he belongs to, the country of which he is a child, and the whole human family of which he is a member, since he is the heir to the work of generations and at the same time a sharer in building the future of those who will come after him in the succession of history. All this constitutes the moral obligation of work.[64]

Thus, to qualify as human work, our activity must be done for the benefit of others—for the benefit of our family, our society,

---

[62] Ibid., 16.
[63] St. Irenaeus, *Adversus haereses*, IV, 20, 7.
[64] John Paul II, *Laborem exercens*, 16.

our country, and all mankind, because our efforts help to build the future for the generations yet to come.

Passive Income and Work

After people learn about this qualification regarding work, they often ask me about a particular money-making program. In short, its goal is to maximize one's passive income by recruiting others to recruit others, who will recruit still others, to buy and sell certain goods or services. They want to know if this type of program qualifies as work.

First, it is important to note that there is nothing inherent in passive income that disqualifies it from being work. Passive income is usually generated by investing in entities whose activities are undertaken in order to benefit others. In these instances, it qualifies as work.

Second, if the main goal of the program is to provide beneficial goods and services, it also likely qualifies. A good test of this is how the program compensates its participants. Is what they are paid primarily based on the amount of goods and services they provide, or on the number of levels of people they recruit?

If the majority of their time—and the bulk of their training—is devoted to recruiting more levels, there may be a problem. In that case, they should discern what benefit, if any, recruiting multiple levels of people—whose primary purpose is to recruit still more levels—actually provides. I recommend that anyone in this type of program begin with prayer, asking God for wisdom[65] regarding their involvement in it.

---

[65] " If any of you lacks wisdom, let him ask God, who gives to all men generously and without reproaching, and it will be given him" (James 1:5).

A Proper Attitude toward Work

Regarding work, then, a good examination of conscience for all
of us is to ask two questions:

✢ Does my work benefit others?

✢ Is benefiting others my primary motivation for undertaking it?

In this context, the meaning of St. Paul's admonitions is clear:

> She who is self-indulgent is dead even while she lives.
> Command this, so that they may be without reproach. If
> any one does not provide for his relatives, and especially
> for his own family, he has disowned the faith and is worse
> than an unbeliever. (1 Tim. 5:6–8)

> Let each of you look not only to his own interests, but
> also to the interests of others. (Phil. 2:4)

> Give no opportunity to the devil. Let the thief no longer
> steal, but rather let him labor, doing honest work with
> his hands, so that he may be able to give to those in need.
> (Eph. 4:27–28)

Vatican II added: "Man ... cannot fully find himself except
through a sincere gift of himself."[66]

After married life, work is a primary way in which we are
called to find our self through making a sincere gift of our self.
Thus, we are exhorted to work diligently and without complaint:
"Whatever your task, work heartily, as serving the Lord" (Col.
3:23). "Do all things without grumbling or questioning" (Phil.
2:14).

---

[66] Paul VI, *Gaudium et spes*, 24.

To Work Is to Share in God's Creation

What About the Disabled Person?

If work is so essential to our humanity, what does that mean for the disabled person? John Paul II addressed this when he said that to deny them the opportunity to work is a serious form of discrimination by the strong and healthy against the weak:

> The disabled person is one of us and participates fully in the same humanity that we possess. It would be radically unworthy of man, and a denial of our ... humanity, to admit ... to work, only those who are fully functional. To do so would be to practice a *serious form of discrimination*, that of the strong and healthy against the weak and sick.[67]

Thus we have a responsibility to develop effective training programs and appropriate work opportunities so that disabled people can obtain jobs that are suited to them:

> The various bodies involved in the world of labor ... should ... foster the right of disabled people to professional training and work, so that they can be given a productive activity suited to them ... *that disabled people may be offered work according to their capabilities*, for this is demanded by their dignity as persons.[68]

Rather than being cut off from work, and thus made dependent on society, disabled people should be respected and called to contribute to both their families and communities through meaningful work:

---

[67] John Paul II, *Laborem exercens*, 22, emphasis in the original.
[68] Ibid., emphasis in the original.

It is to be hoped that a correct concept of labor ... will make it possible for disabled people to feel that they are not cut off from the working world or dependent upon society, but that they are full-scale [members], useful, respected for their human dignity and called to contribute to the progress and welfare of their families and of the community according to their particular capacities.[69]

Work ≠ a Paycheck

Many people work without receiving a paycheck. The mother who stays home to care for her children, a college student who volunteers at a reading program for kids, a person who visits the elderly in a nursing home, the retiree who watches grandchildren after school, the relative who cares for a family member who is incapable of working because of a severe mental or physical impairment, the jobless person who works hard at looking for a new job and meanwhile makes himself useful to others in all sorts of ways — all of these people engage in legitimate forms of work. Each of them is making a sincere gift of himself for the benefit of others. Each, as John Paul II put it, is working "in all the many meanings of the word."[70]

Mass, Miracles, and Manual Labor

Have you ever wondered why, at Mass, bread and wine are used for Holy Communion? First, of course, it is because that is what Jesus instituted at the Last Supper. But why did He choose bread and wine? Why not grain and grapes instead? They are basically the same thing, aren't they?

[69] Ibid.
[70] Ibid., 16.

To Work Is to Share in God's Creation

As John Paul II pointed out, "by means of work man shares in the work of creation."[71] This principle even applies to the Mass. So part of the reason that we use bread and wine in the Mass, instead of grain and grapes, is because bread and wine both require the addition of the work of human hands. God is so committed to our sharing in His divine work that even the Mass cannot take place without it. We see this principle repeated throughout Scripture: no work (i.e., no human participation), no miracle.

The Wedding at Cana

Jesus' first miracle was to turn water into wine. The wedding party at Cana had run out of wine so Mary asked Jesus to intervene. She told the servants, "Do whatever he tells you" (John 2:5). The story continues:

> Now six stone jars were standing there, for the Jewish rites of purification, each holding twenty or thirty gallons. Jesus said to them, "Fill the jars with water." And they filled them up to the brim. (John 2:6–7)

Consider the amount of work that this involved:
+ Six jars averaging 25 gallons each = about 150 gallons of water
+ A gallon of water weighs a little over 8.3 pounds[72]
+ Thus, the miracle involved approximately 1,250 pounds of water.

This took place in ancient Israel; there were no water faucets or hoses. The only way for the servants to get that water was to

---

[71] John Paul II, *Laborem exercens*, 25.
[72] "How Many Pounds in a Gallon," http://howmanypoundsin agallon.com/.

go to a well, lower an empty bucket, draw it up when it was full, carry it back to the feast, and pour it into a jar—all 1,250 pounds of it, one bucket at a time. That certainly constitutes work! It is another example of the necessity of the work of human hands.

Moses and the Bronze Serpent

We find the same principle in the book of Numbers. Fiery serpents had invaded the Israelite's camp and began killing people—everyone who was bitten died.

> So Moses prayed for the people. And the LORD said to Moses, "Make a fiery serpent and set it on a pole, and everyone who is bitten, when he looks at it, will live." So Moses made a bronze serpent and put it on a pole. And if a serpent bit anyone, he would look at the bronze serpent and live. (Num. 21:7–9, ESV)

In order to do this, they had to:
+ obtain bronze
+ design and build a casting mold for a serpent
+ stoke a fire hot enough to melt bronze
+ pour the molten bronze into the mold
+ let it cool, remove it from the mold, and file off the excess metal
+ obtain a pole and make a way to connect a serpent to it
+ secure the serpent to the pole
+ dig a hole, or provide some other means of support, for the pole
+ erect and stabilize the pole

In other words, it involved a lot of work. Even those who were to be healed had to work—they had to go to a place where they could see the bronze serpent and then look at it.

To Work Is to Share in God's Creation

Elijah and the Widow

During a time of famine, the prophet Elijah was sent by God to Syria, where he was miraculously fed by a poor widow, as recounted in the first book of Kings. The widow of Zarephath also worked as part of the miracle God performed for her (1 Kings 17:8–16). She participated in the miracle that kept her, her son, and the prophet Elijah alive throughout a severe famine. She had only enough oil and flour left to make a final meal for her and her son before they died. Yet, because she obeyed God and first worked for the benefit of another, in this case, the prophet Elijah, God caused her supply of oil and flour to be miraculously replenished, every day, until the end of the famine.

Feeding the Five Thousand

Returning to the New Testament, one of the only miracles reported in all four Gospels is Jesus' feeding of the five thousand. Consider the amount of human work that went into that momentous miracle:

+ Grain was planted, tended, harvested, separated, and ground into flour.
+ Bread was mixed, kneaded, and baked.
+ Fish were caught, cleaned, and cooked.
+ Bread and fish were prepared as a meal.
+ A boy offered this meal, as a gift, to the apostles.
+ The five thousand were divided into groups.
+ Jesus blessed the food and broke it into pieces.
+ The apostles distributed the pieces to the groups.
+ Finally, the leftovers were gathered so that nothing would go to waste.

Each of these steps involved a significant amount of human work.

Jesus exercised this principle throughout his ministry — "Take up your pallet and walk" (Mark 2:9; John 5:8); "Stretch out your hand" (Matt. 12:13; Mark 3:5; Luke 6:10); "Go, wash in the pool of Siloam" (John 9:7); "Take away the stone" (John 11:39); and so forth — and, as noted, it runs through all of Scripture. As a rule, God asks us to play an important part in the work He does, and if we don't do our part, He doesn't work the miracle.

No Work, No Miracle — Kadesh-barnea and Nazareth

In case we are tempted to think that God would work the same miracles regardless of whether we did our part, we can think of the example of the Israelites in the wilderness. Even though they had miraculously escaped from Pharaoh's army by passing through the Red Sea, they later died in the desert without entering the Promised Land. They didn't enter it because they did not do their part. Like Adam and Eve, they let trust in God's goodness toward them die in their hearts. At Kadesh-barnea they chose not to believe in God's provision — in His promise to enable them to conquer the land — and were thus prevented from ever entering it. It was their children who were allowed to enter forty years later (Num. 13–14).

And in the New Testament we read these haunting words regarding the miracles that Jesus did *not* work in Nazareth: "And he did not do many mighty works there, because of their unbelief" (Matt. 13:58; cf. Mark 6:5–6).

If we don't do our part, if we don't believe and thus do the work God gives us to do,[73] there are always substantial negative consequences.

---

[73] "This is the work of God, that you believe in him whom he has sent" (John 6:29). "Why do you call me 'Lord, Lord,' and not do what I tell you?" (Luke 6:46).

To Work Is to Share in God's Creation

Absolutely Indispensable, Totally Insufficient

What these examples demonstrate is that our work — our part — is absolutely indispensable. If we don't contribute, God doesn't do the rest. The dignity He has given us includes the fact that our choices matter — that our actions, or inaction, can and do make a difference.

The second thing that each of these examples demonstrates is that our efforts, by themselves, are totally insufficient. The widow knew it wasn't her baking that caused the flour and oil to last; those servants who hauled the water didn't think that it was their efforts that turned it into wine; and the boy knew that his small lunch could not even begin to feed the multitude.

God's love for us is so great that He has called us into a genuine partnership with Him. As His children, we are not meant to be passive observers in life. Through our work, we are called to be active participants in God's ongoing work of creation: "See what great love the Father has lavished on us, that we should be called children of God! And that is what we are!" (1 John 3:1, NIV).

❖

Summary: To Work Is to Share in God's Creation

❖ The first thing God did in Scripture was to work. Thus, in addition to being a God of relationship, He is a God of work.

❖ His work — undertaken for our benefit — is a manifestation of His love.

❖ Created in God's image, we are made to work.

❖ And our work, like His, should benefit others.

✢ God gave us work before the Fall, so work is not a punishment for sin.

✢ Work is a gift from God that enables us to reflect His image fully. As such, it is a primary way to live out our humanity—we cannot be fully human without work.

✢ Thus we have a responsibility regarding disabled people:
  › to provide them with effective training programs
  › and appropriate work opportunities
  › that are suited to them
  › so that they can contribute to their families and societies
  › rather than making them dependent on society

✢ Not to fulfill this responsibility is a serious form of discrimination of the strong and healthy against the weak.

✢ Through work we:
  › live in the image of God
  › become fully human
  › find ourselves through a sincere gift of ourselves
  › share in God's work of creation

✢ Although our work is absolutely indispensable, apart from God it is also totally insufficient.

In the next chapter we will consider how everything we have looked at thus far helps to define Christian charity.

Truth 5

Charity Is Required to Love God and Man

❖

*To love someone is to desire that person's good
and to take effective steps to secure it.*

—Pope Benedict XVI, *Caritas in Veritate*, 7

As St. Thomas Aquinas observed, "virtue lies in the mean between two extremes."[74] Perhaps nowhere is this more apparent than in the application of Catholic teaching regarding charity. A misunderstanding of Aquinas's simple principle may be the root cause of much of the confusion and dissension among well-meaning people on this topic.

Everything we have explored so far has led to this chapter. Since God, at the very essence of His being, is love, and we are made in His image, we too must convey love. We must practice charity.

This theme runs through nearly all of the Vatican II documents. For example:

[74] St. Thomas Aquinas, *Summa Theologica*, I-II, Q. 64, art. 1.

The greatest commandment in the law is to love God with one's whole heart and one's neighbor as oneself (cf. Matt. 22:37–40). Christ made this commandment of love of neighbor His own and enriched it with a new meaning. For He wanted to equate Himself with His brethren as the object of this love when He said, "As long as you did it for one of these, the least of My brethren, you did it for Me" (Matt. 25:40). "By this will all men know that you are My disciples, if you have love for one another" (John 13:35)....

For this reason, pity for the needy and the sick and works of charity and mutual aid intended to relieve human needs of every kind are held in highest honor by the Church....

It is altogether necessary that one should consider in one's neighbor the image of God in which he has been created, and also Christ the Lord to Whom is really offered whatever is given to a needy person.[75]

The greatest commandment is to love God. And since He is already perfectly blessed in Himself (CCC 1), He has no need of anything that we could give Him. Yet love is self-giving for the benefit of another; thus Jesus makes it clear that one of the most real and practical ways we are to love God (who has no need) is by loving others (created in His image), who do have needs.

This is so true that one of Jesus' closest followers went on to say that it is impossible to love God if we don't love our neighbor:

[F]or he who does not love his brother whom he has seen, cannot love God whom he has not seen. And this commandment

---

we have from him, that he who loves God should love his brother also. (1 John 4:20–21)

This point is so crucial that Jesus made it a criterion for entering heaven (see Matt. 25:34–46). In the parable of the sheep and the goats, He said that anyone who meets his neighbor's needs actually meets Jesus' needs in the process, and that anyone who ignores his neighbor's needs ignores Jesus. He concluded with a promise that those who meet their neighbor's needs will receive a rich welcome into heaven and that those who ignore them will not gain entrance.

Why the Confusion?

Scripture makes this point so clearly that all Christians of every time, place, culture, and denomination have taught it. Since that is the case, what is it about this teaching that causes confusion? Pope Benedict XVI captured it succinctly when he noted that: "To love someone is to desire that person's good *and* to take effective steps to secure it."[76] Here we see that love is much more than a feeling — it requires three things of us, the first of which is to desire that person's good.

But desire alone is not enough. The apostle James spoke of the second requirement:

> If a brother or sister is poorly clothed and in lack of daily food, and one of you says to them, "Go in peace, be warmed and filled," without giving them the things needed for the body, what does it profit? (James 2:15–16)

The second requirement, then, is to do something, to take steps to secure that good.

---

[76] Benedict XVI, *Caritas in veritate*, 7, emphasis added.

Yet even that is not enough. Not just any action, any steps, will do. The third requirement is that the steps we take must be effective. They must actually meet the underlying need.

An Example — The Unemployed

Our neighbor is created in the image of God, just as we are. Thus, our charity toward him must be consistent with that image. As noted earlier, that image includes both relationship and work. So, in order to develop fully as a human being, our neighbor needs the opportunity to work. Thus, he needs the opportunity to "find himself through a sincere gift of himself."

The same principles that we discovered in the previous chapter regarding disabled people and work apply here. All of our neighbors need the opportunity to work for the benefit of others — their families, communities, societies, and mankind as a whole.[77] Each and every one of them has a unique gift — a unique contribution — to make. This is why the Church teaches the following:

> Being out of work or dependent on public or private assistance for a prolonged period undermines the freedom and creativity of the person and his family and social relationships, causing great psychological and spiritual suffering.[78]

Please read those words again: *undermines the freedom and creativity of the person and his family and social relationships, causing great psychological and spiritual suffering.*

Thus, while providing long-term public or private assistance may make us feel good, it is not true charity. Leaving people

---

[77] John Paul II, *Laborem exercens*, 16.
[78] Benedict XVI, *Caritas in veritate*, 25.

dependent on society is not loving them. It harms their humanity and denies the image of God within them because it fails to value the unique contributions that only they can make. So the Church adds:

> Help [must] be given in such a way that the recipients may gradually be freed from dependence on outsiders and become self-sufficient.[79]

This led Benedict XVI to note:

> Assistance ... is always designed to achieve their emancipation, because it fosters freedom and participation through assumption of responsibility.[80]

In order to apply the Church's teaching on charity with regard to the unemployed, therefore, we must take action that:

✦ assists in meeting their immediate, short-term needs
✦ gradually frees them from the need for that assistance
✦ leads them to assume responsibility for themselves and their families
✦ enables them to become self-sufficient

Anything that stops short of this is not true charity. Thus, John Paul II further noted:

> The Church has always been present and active among the needy, offering them material assistance in ways that neither humiliate nor reduce them to mere objects of assistance, but which help them to escape their precarious situation by promoting their dignity as persons.[81]

---

[79] Paul VI, *Apostolicam actuositatem*, 8.
[80] Benedict XVI, *Caritas in veritate*, 57.
[81] John Paul II, *Centesimus annus*, 49.

Voluntarily Unemployment

This is why the Church has always distinguished between those who are unemployed through no fault of their own[82] and those who simply choose not to work. Only in this context do the sobering words of St. Paul make sense:

> May the Lord direct your hearts to the love of God and to the steadfastness of Christ. Now we command you, brethren, in the name of our Lord Jesus Christ, that you keep away from any brother who is living in idleness.... For you yourselves know how you ought to imitate us; we were not idle when we were with you, we did not eat any one's bread without paying, but with toil and labor we worked night and day, that we might not burden any of you ... to give you ... an example to imitate.
>
> For even when we were with you, we gave you this command: If any one will not work, let him not eat. For we hear that some of you are living in idleness ... not doing any work. Now such persons we command and exhort in the Lord Jesus Christ to do their work ... and to earn their own living.... If anyone refuses to obey what we say in this letter, note that man, and have nothing to do with him, that he may be ashamed. Do not look on him as an enemy, but warn him as a brother. (2 Thess. 3:5–15)

Paul begins by directing us to the love of God and to Christ's patience. He is telling us that what follows comes straight from, and is a practical application of, God's love, stating it as an emphatic command from God ("Now we command you, brethren, in the name of our Lord Jesus Christ ...").

---

[82] John XXIII, *Pacem in terris*, 11.

And what does he command us to do regarding those who choose not to work?

> Keep away from any brother who is living in idleness.... If anyone will not work, let him not eat.... Note that man, and have nothing to do with him, that he may be ashamed.

Out of love, out of sincere concern for the good of those who choose not to work, we are commanded to:

✢ keep away from them
✢ let them go hungry
✢ have nothing to do with them
✢ allow them to become ashamed

Again, all of this is to be done from our hearts, directed in the love of God, for the good of the other, the other who cannot become fully human, who cannot fully develop as a human being, who can never truly find himself until he makes a sincere gift of himself, until he makes his own unique, irreplaceable contribution, in the image of God, for others. That is why Paul concludes by reminding us "not [to] look on him as an enemy, but [to] warn him as a brother."

Better to Be Underemployed?

I've heard some say, "It's better to be unemployed than to take a job that I'm overqualified for, especially if I can receive more money on unemployment than I can earn from working a menial job." It's almost as though God anticipated that line of reasoning in the above passage:

> For you yourselves know how you ought to imitate us; we were not idle when we were with you, we did not eat any one's bread without paying, but with toil and labor we

worked night and day, that we might not burden any of you ... to give you in our conduct an example to imitate.

Paul was one of the greatest theologians who ever lived and one of the most remarkable missionaries of all time. He is credited with having written nearly half of the New Testament. Yet "with toil and labor," he said, "we worked night and day, that we might not burden any of you ... not eat any one's bread without paying ... to give you an example to imitate."

What did Paul do night and day to give us an example to imitate and to ensure that he didn't eat anyone's bread without paying for it? How did this great theologian, missionary, and author toil and labor in order to eat? He did a job that most would say was "beneath him," one for which he was undoubtedly overqualified. He engaged in manual labor—he made tents.[83]

As if to drive this point home, Paul added:

Concerning love of the brethren ... we exhort you ... more and more ... to work with your hands ... and be dependent on nobody. (1 Thess. 4:9–12)

This requirement—that we work in order to meet our needs and those of others, particularly our families—is so essential to Christian teaching that Paul added that whoever fails to do so has "disowned the faith" and is even "worse than an unbeliever" (1 Tim. 5:8).

Old Testament Food Stamps

In the Old Testament, we find a curious series of directives regarding care for the poor and the immigrant ("sojourner"). These

---

[83] "[A]nd because he was of the same trade he stayed with them, and they worked, for by trade they were tentmakers" (Acts 18:3).

directives are so unusual, so counter to our modern mindset, that it's tempting to skim past them—to believe that they no longer have any application for us. Yet they are so important that God restated them on at least three separate occasions:

> When you reap the harvest of your land, you shall not reap your field to its very border, neither shall you gather the gleanings after your harvest. And you shall not strip your vineyard bare, neither shall you gather the fallen grapes of your vineyard; you shall leave them for the poor and for the sojourner: I am the LORD your God. (Lev. 19:9–10; 23:22; cf. Deut. 24:19–21)

It is almost as if God was concerned that we wouldn't understand this the first time, or the second, or even the third. I say this because he later added an entire book (Ruth) in which the practical application of these directives was played out, ultimately leading to the birth of Jesus Himself (see Matt. 1:5).

In reality, these simple directives contain the mean between two extremes we referred to in the opening of this chapter.

First Extreme

Why didn't God tell the Israelites to harvest to the edges of their fields and to go back over them a second time to make sure that they got everything? Then they could have given a portion of the harvest to those in need. Why this curious command, instead, to leave the edges and gleanings for the poor and the sojourners to gather for themselves?

You may have already discerned the answer: gathering the crops for them would take away from them the "opportunity to participate" in the work, and would thus be a denial of their dignity.

These directives safeguard against one extreme: that of seeing those in need as hapless victims to whom we should provide food, clothing, and shelter, without any condition, for as long as they want. But this extreme, over "a prolonged period," destroys the very humanity of the person who is provided for. Intended or not (actions speak louder than words), it sends the clear message that the person thus "helped" has no value to add and that they are incapable of making a genuine contribution, and ultimately it "undermines both their freedom and dignity" and thus leads to their disintegration as human beings.

Second Extreme

These directives also safeguard against the other extreme: that of thinking, "What's mine is mine. I've earned it, so I can keep it all for myself." This mindset includes the inclination to see the poor person or the immigrant as nothing more than an unproductive nuisance who is "somebody else's problem." In short, these directives guard the potential giver from greed, self-centeredness, and a lack of compassion. This extreme is so problematic that Jesus told at least three stories to warn against it—the stories of the rich young ruler (Matt. 19:16–26), of Lazarus and the rich man (Luke 16:19–31), and of the rich fool who built bigger barns for himself (Luke 12:16–21).

We are to care for, and to meet the needs of, the poor and the sojourner. We are to fulfill that great commandment to love our neighbor as ourselves. Thus, we are, in a very real and practical sense, our "brother's keeper" (Gen. 4:9). But we are to do all of this in a way that does not do for others what they can, and should, *do for themselves*.[84] It reminds us that the words from

[84] Benedict XVI, *Caritas in veritate*, 57.

Genesis still apply—"In the sweat of your face you shall eat bread" (Gen. 3:19). And that applies to all of us, including the poor, the unemployed, and the immigrant.

What God Values

From these directives we can see that God values our humanity—made in His image—far more than He values our productivity, our comfort, or our material success. It would be more productive to gather to the edges of the fields while we were already working in them. It would make more financial sense as well. After all, if no needy person ever showed up, the harvest we left in the field would go to waste. At least if we harvested it ourselves, and set some of it aside to give to the poor, it wouldn't spoil or get eaten by birds. Better yet, if we harvested everything ourselves, we could sell the excess and donate that money to the needy. That way, nothing would go to waste.

But as we've seen, there is something much more important than efficiency at stake. The inherent value and dignity of people—both the giver and the recipient—is what matters. Thus, the call for us to offer the needy "material assistance in ways that neither humiliate nor reduce them to mere objects of assistance, but which help them to escape their precarious situation by promoting their dignity as persons," supersedes other considerations.

Even from a purely pragmatic point of view, this practice makes sense. By gathering the food for themselves, people keep physically fit, develop practical skills, demonstrate their work ethic to potential employers, and continue to grow in the good habits of industriousness[85] and responsibility, as Pope Benedict

---

[85] "Without this consideration it is impossible to understand ... why industriousness should be a virtue: for virtue, as a moral

pointed out.[86] In short, rather than disintegrating as human beings, they continue to develop. They grow in the virtues of work and increase their ability to find work.

Is This Teaching Still Relevant?

Again, it can be very tempting to think that these Old Testament directives are no longer relevant today. After all, at the time they were written, almost everyone lived in an agricultural society, so this form of charity was a viable option. Today the majority of the world's population live in urban areas. For example, 82 percent of the citizens in North America live in cities.[87] Thus, many of the world's poor live so far from any agricultural activity that they couldn't glean from the fields even if they wanted to.

To conclude that these principles no longer apply would be a grave mistake, however. Human nature and its intrinsic dignity have not changed. The truth—that each of us has a unique contribution to make—has not changed. Our need to provide for our families has not changed. So how do we apply these directives today?

Dallas, Denver, and New Delhi

Dallas

First, we can support private charities that follow these principles. For example, Christian Community Action,[88] in Dallas–Fort

---

habit, is something whereby man becomes good as man." John Paul II, *Laborem exercens*, 9.

[86] Benedict XVI, *Caritas in veritate*, 57.

[87] United Nations, *World Urbanization Prospects*, 2014, p. 1, https://esa.un.org/unpd/wup/Publications/Files/WUP2014-Highlights.pdf.

[88] Christian Community Action, http://ccahelps.org/about-us/.

Worth, Texas, has been creatively doing so for more than forty years. When someone asks them for money, CCA doesn't just give them a handout. Instead, they pay the person to take classes on budgeting and basic financial principles. If someone comes looking for food or clothing, they pay them in vouchers (good for items in CCA's store), to attend training in things such as healthy shopping and good nutrition. As one of their spokespersons put it:

> CCA's mission is to demonstrate Christ's love and restore poor people's dignity while also teaching responsibility. Our goal is to change lives.... By allowing them to select their own food and requiring them to budget their own voucher money, we help them reach the point where they don't need us anymore.[89]

Additionally, they provide training that enables people to get, and keep, real jobs. For example, they offer courses in English as a second language, GED preparation, computer skills, financial management, resume writing, interview skills, and how to find a job.[90]

Denver
Statistics indicate that drug and alcohol abuse play a major role in unemployment, homelessness, and incarceration. In fact, when

---

[89] "A Dallas coalition of churches and businesses care for people by teaching them responsibility." Candi Cushman, "Their Brothers' Teacher," *World* 16, no. 19 (May 19, 2001), https://world.wng.org/.

[90] "Crisis and Support Services: Essential Training and Life Skills," Christian Community Action, http://ccahelps.org/cca-programs/crisis-support-services/.

I worked for Prison Fellowship Ministries, the Colorado Department of Corrections stated that 73 to 78 percent of those behind bars were there, either directly or indirectly, because of drug- or alcohol-related issues.[91] Two Denver programs apply the above principles to these problems.

Step 13 is a nationally recognized residential recovery program for men.[92] Its tag line is "A Hand Up. Not a Handout." Founded in 1996, Step 13 has developed a remarkably successful program that frees men from these addictions, teaches them marketable job skills, and eventually leads them to independence.

Joshua Station does similar work with families. As they explain:

> Joshua Station ... provides a transitional home for homeless families, helping them develop the skills and self-sufficiency needed to secure stable housing. Joshua Station requires counseling and community involvement, helps families make goals for their future, and educates families in life skills like budgeting and parenting. The station is committed to extending grace and mercy while holding families accountable for behavior.[93]

---

[91] "In 2006, alcohol and other drugs were involved in 78% of violent crimes, 83% of property crimes, and 77% of public order, immigration or weapons offenses and probation/parole violations." "Behind Bars II: Substance Abuse and America's Prison Population," National Center on Addiction and Substance Abuse, February 2010, http://www.centeronaddiction.org/.

[92] "President George H. W. Bush designated Step 13 one of his 'Thousand Points of Light.' ABC's 20/20 and John Stossel featured Bob and the simple, yet effective approach to helping residents become sober and self-reliant." "Bob Coté, Founder of Step 13," Step 13 website, https://www.step13.org/Founder/index.asp.

[93] Alisha Harris, "Effective Compassion: Mile-High Hope," *World Magazine*, September 1, 2007.

Charity Is Required to Love God and Man

New Delhi

Microlenders apply these Old Testament principles internationally. Heifer International[94] provides "livestock loans" to poor families. The animals provide both food and reliable income, since agricultural products such as milk, eggs, and honey can be traded or sold at market, further enabling these families to rise out of poverty and to become self-sufficient. Those who are helped subsequently pay back the "loans," enabling Heifer to assist still more families.

Kiva has been a leading provider of microloans in India and throughout the third world.[95] Microloans are very small monetary loans that enable potential entrepreneurs to start their own businesses. Microlenders typically focus their lending on vulnerable and marginalized people in third-world countries, such as widows and refugees. The loans are used to purchase items such as sewing machines, fishing equipment, or bikes that enable the borrowers to start a small business.[96] The loans are eventually paid back, enabling the organization to help even more families.

In Common

What each of these charities has in common and the reason organizations like these warrant our support is that they closely adhere to the Church's teachings regarding charity:

[94] Morgan Winsor, "Bill Gates Launches Chicken Initiative to Tackle Poverty in Africa," ABC News, June 9, 2016, http://abcnews.go.com/Business/bill-gates-launches-chicken-initiative-tackle-poverty-africa/story?id=39722297.

[95] "Financial Inclusion Challenge Finalist: Kiva," *Wall Street Journal*, June 15, 2015, http://www.wsj.com/video/financial-inclusion-challenge-finalist-kiva/D7440226-C296-427E-A449-8F849D3D4D06.html AND www.kiva.org.

[96] "The Story of Microfinance," KickLoans, http://kickloans.org/the-story-of-microfinance/.

✣ All of them "desire [the] person's good and … take effective steps to secure it."

✣ They are "present and active among the needy, offering them material assistance in ways that neither humiliate nor reduce them to mere objects of assistance, but which help them to escape their precarious situation by promoting their dignity as persons."

✣ Their help "is given in such a way that the recipients may gradually be freed from dependence on outsiders and become self-sufficient."

✣ And their assistance "is always designed to achieve [the recipients'] emancipation, because it fosters freedom and participation through assumption of responsibility."

✤

Summary: Charity Is Required to Love God and Man

✣ Charity is an absolute necessity for all Christians, so much so that Jesus makes our practice of it a criterion for entering heaven.

✣ Genuine charity requires one to do three things:
  › Desire the other person's good.
  › Take steps to secure that good.
  › Do so effectively to address the underlying problem.

✣ Thus, in regard to the unemployed, our charity must:
  › Assist in meeting their immediate, short-term needs.
  › Gradually free them from needing that assistance.
  › Lead them to assume responsibility for themselves and their families.
  › Ultimately enable them to become self-sufficient.

Charity Is Required to Love God and Man

✣ This is true because "being out of work or dependent on public or private assistance for a prolonged period undermines the freedom and creativity of the person and his family and social relationships, causing great psychological and spiritual suffering."

✣ Thus, the Church has always distinguished between those who are unemployed through no fault of their own and those who simply choose not to work.

  › We are to assist those who are unemployed through no fault of their own in the ways listed above.

  › We are not to provide for the needs of those who choose not to work—that would be to deny their value and dignity and undermine their ability to live in God's image.

✣ Because we are all created in God's image, every person has a unique contribution to make—a unique value that only he can add—and true charity's goal is to help him do so.

Truth 6

Catholic Social Teaching Is Rooted in Truth

Without truth, charity degenerates into sentimentality. Love be-
comes an empty shell, to be filled in an arbitrary way. In a culture
without truth, this is the fatal risk facing love. It falls prey to . . .
subjective emotions and opinions, the word "love" is abused and
distorted, to the point where it comes to mean the opposite.[97]

—Pope Benedict XVI, *Caritas in veritate*, 3

Pope Benedict's words, above, bring us back to the need to tackle the root causes of poverty:

It is imperative ... that ... not only the effects but also the causes of these ills must be removed.[98]

The Church's social teaching requires us to move beyond just addressing the effects of poverty and to help remove the root causes. To clarify, what I am about to share applies specifically to poverty in first-world countries; later we'll look at the third world.

The social sciences have discovered a lot about the causes of first-world poverty. But what they've discovered isn't glamorous

[97] Benedict XVI, *Caritas in veritate*, 3.
[98] Paul VI, *Apostolicam actuositatem*, 8.

and doesn't call for new government bureaucracies or taxes. There aren't any lobbyist or special-interest groups who gain from their implementation. In fact, they are fairly boring—they never make the nightly news and don't stir much passion. This means it is still more important for people who are concerned about the welfare of others—people who sincerely care about removing the causes of poverty—to be actively and persuasively involved in implementing these discoveries.

William Galston is the Chair of Governance Studies and a senior fellow at the prestigious Brookings Institute. He was previously the Saul Stern Professor and Dean at the School of Public Policy at the University of Maryland. Additionally he was the deputy assistant for domestic policy to President Bill Clinton and was employed by both the Al Gore and Walter Mondale presidential campaigns.[99] In short, he both knows what he's talking about and is anything but a political or social conservative, which makes his findings all the more interesting.

In collaboration with Ron Haskins, his research found that anyone can reduce their chances of ending up in long-term poverty—by up to 90 percent—through following these three simple steps:[100]

1. Graduate from high school.
2. Get and keep a full-time job.
3. Do not have children until you are married, and wait until you are at least twenty-one to get married.

---

[99] "William A. Galston," Brookings Institute, http://www.brookings.edu/experts/galstonw?view=bio.

[100] Ron Haskins, "Three Simple Rules Poor Teens Should Follow to Join the Middle Class," Brookings, March 13, 2013, http://www.brookings.edu/research/opinions/2013/03/13-join-middle-class-haskins.

Only 8 percent of those who followed these steps are poor, while 79 percent of those who have not followed them end up in poverty.[101] Thus, our primary focus, in terms of helping the poor, should be to teach these simple steps—and to provide the training and skills needed to live them. All of this echoes John Paul II in *Laborem exercens* regarding the importance of the virtue of industriousness,[102] and the relationships between work, virtue, and family life.[103]

Obesity versus Malnutrition and Starvation

All poverty is not the same, so there can be no one-size-fits-all solution. This is another reason for the frequent confusion and dissension over this issue among well-meaning people. For example, whereas obesity and obesity-related diseases are the number-one health problem among the poor within the United States,[104] starvation, malnutrition, and their related maladies are the primary health problems for those living in poverty within the third world.[105]

---

[101] "3 Life Choices to Prevent Poverty," Time for Excellence, January 28, 2015, https://lifesmartblog.com/.

[102] John Paul II, *Laborem exercens*, 9.

[103] Ibid., 10.

[104] "Obesity Number One Health Problem in US, Says CDC," U.S. Centers for Disease Control and Prevention, January 30, 2004, http://www.worldhealth.net/. "In contrast to international trends, people in America who live in the most poverty-dense counties are those most prone to obesity. Counties with poverty rates of >35% have obesity rates 145% greater than wealthy counties." James A. Levine, "Poverty and Obesity in the U.S.," American Diabetes Association, http://www.ncbi.nlm.nih.gov/pmc/articles/PMC3198075/.

[105] Anaup Shah, "Causes of Hunger Are Related to Poverty," *Global Issues*, October 3, 2010, http://www.globalissues.org/article/7/causes-of-hunger-are-related-to-poverty.

Unfortunately, not recognizing the truth of these very different realities can lead well-meaning people and organizations to take actions that—as Pope Benedict warned—can be ineffective at best, and *arbitrary, distorted*, and *the opposite* of love, at worst.[106]

Isn't It the Thought That Counts?

I know firsthand from my time working with Prison Fellowship Ministries that those involved in outreach to the poor sincerely want to help; they believe they are practicing charity when they give food to poor people. Yet charity requires us to ask if giving free food to able-bodied people of working age, many of whom—according to the statistics—are suffering from obesity, meets the Church's definition of charity. Does it ensure that "the recipients may gradually be freed from dependence on outsiders and become self-sufficient"?[107] Is it seeking to "remove the causes" of their poverty?[108] Is it "designed to achieve their emancipation, or to foster freedom and participation through assumption of responsibility"?[109]

First-World versus Third-World Poverty

Again, these situations arise when we practice appropriate third-world charitable activities (feeding those suffering from malnutrition or starvation through no fault of their own), in a first-world poverty situation in which able-bodied people, for various reasons, freely choose not to work.

---

[106] Benedict XVI, *Caritas in veritate*, 3.
[107] Paul VI, *Apostolicam actuositatem*, 8.
[108] Ibid.
[109] Benedict XVI, *Caritas in veritate*, 57.

Catholic Social Teaching Is Rooted in Truth

What the inner-city poor I met that day needed most was not more free food but to understand their dignity as human beings. They needed to be shown that they have value to add—to their families and to their communities. They needed to be helped to recognize that they each have a unique contribution to make. To help them—according to Catholic social teaching—we first need to assist them in understanding these truths, to understand their incredible worth and dignity as human beings made in the image of God.

Then, as with the charities mentioned in chapter 5, we need to provide whatever education, job training, and skills are needed for them to become productive members of society—for them to "fully develop their humanity."[110] And, in a modern application of the Old Testament principles we discussed earlier, they need to be given the opportunity to work—to contribute to others in meaningful ways—in order to earn the temporary food, clothing, and shelter they require during the training process. This practical method of charity "respects personal dignity by recognizing in the person [one] who is always capable of giving something to others."[111] It recognizes that the ultimate goal of charitable giving is to enable the recipients to reach their fullest potential as fellow human beings, not to leave them in a state of dependence on others as if they have nothing worthwhile to contribute.

How much more valuable would it be to enlist those same affluent suburbanites to mentor people who want to escape poverty? How much more lasting an impact would it have if they were equipped to help teach these poor people the job and life

---

[110] John Paul II, *Laborem exercens*, 16.
[111] Benedict XVI, *Caritas in veritate*, 57.

skills they need to reach their full potential and thus to truly become "emancipated [from] dependence on outsiders"?[112]

Phil—A Changed Life

Early in my career I worked as a restaurant manager. One day a person from social services came to ask if I'd be willing to participate in a new job-training program. Briefly, I would train one of their staff members to do a job at the restaurant, and that staff member would, in turn, train a mentally or physically challenged young adult to do that job. The trainer (job coach) would work with that person for as long as it took him to be able to perform the job to our standards. I would also need to commit to hire the youth, guaranteeing him a certain number of hours a week once he was fully trained.

I agreed, and the following week they brought in a young man—Phil—to start the program. Although I had initially been excited about the program, the moment I met Phil I began to have doubts. Phil, his job coach, and I spent about thirty-five minutes together as the coach told me a little about Phil and I gave them a tour of the restaurant and walked them through their various job duties. Phil was going to be a dishwasher and busboy, as that's what their job-screening process said would be the best fit for him.

During the entire thirty-five minutes, Phil never made eye contact—even once. I introduced him to several of the waitresses and the rest of my management team, with the same result. In fact, I don't think he said a single word during the entire process, and he never looked up from the floor. After Phil and his coach left, my staff expressed their concerns—which I now shared, only more so since I had approved the program. A short time later the job coach called to reassure me and told me that

---

[112] Paul VI, *Apostolicam actuositatem*, 8.

Phil's behavior had been typical for a first-day trainee in the program. I remained doubtful.

Flash forward three months. It's the same time of day as our first meeting (midafternoon, after the lunch rush), and out in the dining room are sitting almost all the members of my crew. They are smiling, laughing, and enjoying each other's company. And the one who has them laughing the most—with his jokes, stories, and offbeat sense of humor—is Phil. In fact, the reason they are gathered there in the first place is because they are about to go out to a movie and ice cream to celebrate Phil's birthday.

In three short months Phil had gone from being unable to make eye contact to being loved and befriended by the entire crew. And in the process he had become one of my best employees—utterly dependable, genuinely caring, extremely diligent, and as good at his job as anyone I had ever managed. His parents later tried to thank me for giving Phil the job opportunity, but as I told them, Phil was the one who had blessed us.

Joan G. and Others

During my tenure in the restaurant industry I saw this same transformation take place over a dozen times and in diverse cities. People's entire lives were radically improved as they were given the job training they needed and an opportunity to put it to work. Joan G. is one of my favorite examples. She suffered from what we would today recognize as being a mild form of fetal-alcohol syndrome. She lived in a negligent, abusive home and saw no way out. She originally started working as a dishwasher. Because she didn't have a driver's license, she had to rely on public transportation to get to work.

Joan was very responsible and committed to being on time—in fact, she typically arrived ninety minutes early for work. She said that the buses weren't reliable enough for her to risk taking a later one. Even though learning was hard for her and developing new skills took a lot of time, she was very determined. While she waited for her shift to start each day, she would watch the opening crew do their work and ask them questions about what they were doing.

After Joan had been with us for about four months, one of the opening-crew members moved to a different city, so we needed a new opener. Joan asked to be given a chance to earn the position, which would mean more hours and a raise. She said that she wouldn't need any training because she had already memorized all of the opening steps by watching her teammates. We agreed to let her try it for a week, and, as you've probably guessed, she excelled at it—so much so that within six months she was promoted to the opening-team leader position, had gotten her driver's license and a car, and had moved into an apartment with her friend Lisa, the opening waitress.

What about Those Who Can't?

At this point you may be wondering, "What about those who truly can't work? What about those people who are so physically or mentally disabled that they can't perform any job function—any type of work at all? Aren't they fully human too?"

Here again we see the wisdom of the Church's teaching:

> Assistance is offered when individuals or groups are unable to accomplish something on their own, and it ... respects personal dignity by recognizing in the person a subject who is always capable of giving something to others.[113]

---

[113] Benedict XVI, *Caritas in veritate*, 57.

Catholic Social Teaching Is Rooted in Truth

Catholic social teaching absolutely requires us to offer assistance when individuals or groups are unable to accomplish something on their own. Much of Mother Teresa's work among the poorest of the poor was exactly of this type. The order she founded—the Missionaries of Charity—continues that work. They began by walking the streets of Calcutta to find those who were too sick or malnourished to care for themselves. Many were in the last hours of their lives and had been abandoned, left to die alone.

The sisters took them in and treated them with the dignity and respect they deserved as fellow human beings. They provided practical care for them as they cleaned their wounds, washed their diseased bodies, and fed and cared for them until the time of their death. They continue to do this work in cities throughout the world. By their love, these sisters demonstrate the tremendous value of each and every person.

And, when needed, they do the same in first- and second-world countries. In fact they currently serve in more than 130 countries,[114] including the United States, where they run a series of AIDS hospices. That's because all people have an equal, intrinsic value and dignity by virtue of their being made in God's image.[115] And, as such, all deserve our help, especially those who are in most need, as John Paul II noted:

> The parable of the Good Samaritan ... indicates what the relationship of each of us must be towards our suffering neighbor. We are not allowed to "pass by on the other side"

[114] "Mother Teresa: The Nun Who Changed the World—Missionaries of Charity," Learn to Question, http://www.learntoquestion.com/seevak/sites/2012/mother-teresa/missionarycharity.html.
[115] CCC 1934; *Compendium of the Catechism of the Catholic Church*, 412.

indifferently; we must "stop" beside him.... This stopping does not mean curiosity but availability.... The Good Samaritan of Christ's parable does not stop at sympathy and compassion alone.... A Good Samaritan is one who brings help ... help which is, as far as possible, effective.... Suffering, which is present under so many different forms in our human world, is also present in order to unleash love in the human person, that unselfish gift of one's "I" on behalf of other people, especially those who suffer.[116]

Thus the Church has constantly insisted that "everyone is always capable of giving something to others."[117] Even the most disabled person gives others an opportunity "to unleash love ... that unselfish gift of one's 'I' on behalf of other people, especially those who suffer." This truth has led many saints to suggest that God allows some to be rich for the very purpose of giving them the opportunity to grow in charity through their service to the poor and suffering (CCC 1936–1937).

John Paul II reminded us that:

A society will be judged on the basis of how it treats its weakest ... and most vulnerable members [particularly] the unborn and the dying.[118]

Meeting Others' Spiritual Needs

No review of charity and Catholic social teaching would be complete if it failed to mention what the Church says is the "preeminent

---

[116] John Paul II, *Salvifici doloris*, 28–29.

[117] Benedict XVI, *Caritas in veritate*, 57.

[118] John Paul II, Address to the new ambassador of New Zealand, May 25, 2000, 6.

responsibility"[119] of charity. As Joseph Ratzinger, first as cardinal and later as Pope Benedict XVI, put it:

> As disciples of Jesus Christ, we have to give men what they most need—communion with the living God.[120]
>
> Everything depends upon intimate friendship with Jesus[121] ... so the most urgent priority ... is to ... foster the growth of a personal relationship with him.[122]

In this he echoed his predecessor Paul VI who, in the Vatican II Decree on the Apostolate of the Laity, noted:

> This apostolate should reach out to all wherever they may be encountered; it should not exclude any spiritual or temporal benefit which they have the ability to confer. True apostles however, are not content with this activity alone but endeavor to announce Christ to their neighbors by means of the spoken word as well.[123]

This truth is reiterated even more succinctly in the *Compendium of the Catechism of the Catholic Church*, 414: "The sharing of the spiritual goods of faith ... is even more important than sharing material goods."

Thus, for charity to be truly *Catholic*, and for it to conform to the Church's social teaching, it must address man's deepest need and speak to his deepest nature. In addition to meeting his physical needs, it must also address his personal relationship with God, through Christ his Son, and the Church he founded.

---

[119] Paul VI, *Apostolicam actuositatem*, 3.

[120] Cardinal Joseph Ratzinger, *Gospel, Catechesis, Catechism*, p. 41.

[121] Benedict XVI, *Jesus of Nazareth*, vol. 1, p. xii.

[122] Ibid., p. xxiv.

[123] Paul VI, *Apostolicam actuositatem*, 13.

✤✦✤

Summary: Catholic Social Teaching Is Rooted in Truth

✤ Research shows that the chances of entering long-term poverty in the United States can be reduced by up to 90 percent with three simple steps:
  › Graduate from high school.
  › Get and keep a full-time job.
  › Do not have children until you are married, and wait until you are at least twenty-one to get married.
✤ Only 8 percent of those who followed these steps are poor, whereas 80 percent of those who have not followed them end up in poverty.
✤ Thus, to combat poverty in the United States, we need to teach these steps and provide the training and skills needed to live them.
✤ A one-size-fits-all approach to combatting poverty leads to serious problems because first-world poverty and third-world poverty are very different.
  › Obesity and its related diseases are the number-one health problem among the poor in the United States.
  › Starvation and malnutrition are the chief health problems among the poor in the third world.
  › These starkly contrasting realities call for very different forms of charity to address their root causes effectively.
✤ True Catholic charity must also address people's spiritual needs.

Part 3

The Foundational Truths
Applied Publicly

Truth 7

Governing Requires Prudence
for Real Charity to Occur

❖

The principal task of the State is to guarantee . . . security,
so that those who work and produce can enjoy the fruits
of their labors and thus feel encouraged
to work efficiently and honestly.[124]

—Pope St. John Paul II, *Centesimus annus*, 48

The truth we looked at in chapter 5 — that our very humanity requires us to work — is so fundamental that the Church uses it as a primary criterion in defining the role of government:

> Hence the principal task of the State is to guarantee ... security, so that those who work and produce can enjoy the fruits of their labors and thus feel encouraged to work efficiently and honestly.... The State has a duty to sustain business activities by creating conditions which will ensure job opportunities.[125]

[124] John Paul II, *Centesimus annus*, 48.
[125] Ibid.

So the primary tasks of the State are (1) to provide security (law and order and national defense)[126] and (2) to create conditions that ensure job opportunities so that workers can enjoy the fruits of their labor and be encouraged to work more efficiently and honestly.

As Catholics we should support government policies that encourage job growth rather than inhibit it and that best enable workers to enjoy the fruits of their labors.

Stability and economic order are so critical that John Paul II identified a lack of them—along with corrupt politicians, illegal activities, and purely speculative investing—among the chief obstacles to development:

> The absence of stability, together with the corruption of public officials and the spread ... of easy profits deriving from illegal or purely speculative activities, constitutes one of the chief obstacles to development and to the economic order.[127]

The Fruit of Labor

As John Paul II noted, the main purpose of stability and economic order is "that those who work and produce can enjoy the fruits of their labors." Four times in Scripture this principle is stated as variations of the following:

> "You shall not muzzle an ox when it is treading out the grain." Is it for oxen that God is concerned? Does he not speak entirely for our sake? It was written for our

---

[126] CCC 2240, 2242, 2309–2310, 2321.
[127] John Paul II, *Centesimus annus*, 48.

sake, because the plowman should plow in hope and the thresher thresh in hope of a share in the crop.[128]

Thus, a central point in Catholic social teaching is that "the worker deserves his wages" (Luke 10:7; cf. 2 Tim. 2:6).

Whose Money Is Your Money?

Because this teaching is so ubiquitous, it shows up in some unexpected places. For example, most of us are familiar with Jesus' parable of the landowner who hired people to work in his vineyard. He hired people throughout the day—which meant that the workers worked different numbers of hours. Yet, at the end of the day, the owner paid them all a full day's wages. Homilies on this passage tend to focus on generosity, envy, the first being last, and so forth. And all of these are legitimate applications of the story, but I want to draw your attention to one particular statement by the landowner: "Don't I have a right to do what I want with my own money? Or are you envious because I am generous?" (Matt. 20:15, NIV).

In this story, which was told by Christ Himself, the fact that each of us has a right to do what we want with our own money is both taken for granted and central to the story's meaning. If the landowner didn't have a right to do whatever he wanted with his money, the story wouldn't make sense—the parable presupposes that right. And money is the fruit of his labor—the labor of owning, planting, and caring for his vineyard.

The account of Ananias and Sapphira illustrates this truth in a more dramatic way. Many of the early Christians voluntarily sold their property so that they could give money to the

---

[128] 1 Cor. 9:9–10. See also Deut. 25:4; 1 Tim. 5:18; 2 Tim. 2:6.

poor. Ananias and Sapphira wanted to appear generous, so they sold some of their property and donated *part* of the proceeds to the poor. But, in order to look more generous, they claimed to have donated *all* of the proceeds. Here's what the Apostle Peter said when confronting the couple about their land and money: "Didn't it belong to you before it was sold? And after it was sold, wasn't the money at your disposal?" (Acts 5:4, NIV). Here again the Scriptural principle is that your money and property are yours to do with as you choose. They do not belong to the State, the community, the Church, or anyone else — they are yours.

Charity Must Be Voluntary

Charity, by definition, must be voluntary, because it flows from the nature of who God is and who man is. God is love, and love is a free choice to seek the good of another. Thus "man can only find himself through a sincere gift of himself."[129] That is why all charity, all love, must be a sincere gift — and a gift is a gift only if it is freely given.

The apostle Paul reiterated this when he coordinated a charitable donation from the Corinthian church. They had committed to help the poor, and Paul wanted to make sure that in fulfilling their commitment they were doing so freely. Twice he reminded them that their charity should be "a willing gift" and that it shouldn't "be given reluctantly or under compulsion" (2 Cor. 9:5, 7).

Paul J. Glenn, in his *Tour of the Summa* of St. Thomas Aquinas, further developed this point:

> Alms are to be given out of the donor's own property. To use the surplus of a rich neighbor to relieve the needy is

---

[129] Paul VI, *Gaudium et spes*, 24.

to be guilty of theft. The goods of others are not ours to dispose of without their directions or permission.[130]

Commenting on Aquinas' teaching, Pope Leo XIII went so far as to say that, whereas it is true that the Christian has a moral duty to be charitable, "it is a duty, not of justice (save in extreme cases), but of Christian charity—a duty not enforced by human law."[131]

Thus, Christianity understands that the government cannot coerce charity. Neither can it perform charity—only individuals and voluntary associations of individuals can. The government can't make a sincere gift of itself—it has nothing of its own to give. Sadly, many don't understand this. They mistakenly believe that lobbying to raise other people's taxes is somehow an act of charity if that money is earmarked for the poor. But voting to raise other people's taxes (or more rarely, their own) so that the state can give that money to the poor is not charity. It violates every requirement for charity because the money thus obtained:

✢ is not a gift (no one pays taxes as a gift)

✢ is not given freely (particularly by those who didn't vote for it)

✢ does not belong to the giver (the state was not the original owner)

✢ is given under government compulsion (if you doubt that, look at what happens to someone who doesn't pay his taxes)

---

[130] Paul J. Glenn, A *Tour of the Summa*, pt. 2B, 32, http://www.catholictheology.info/summa-theologica/summa-part2B.php?q=256.

[131] Leo XIII, *Rerum novarum*, 22.

Socialism and Communism

These teachings begin to explain why the Church has consistently warned against the dangers of socialism and communism[132] and why she has condemned both systems as illegitimate and inhumane. Pope Leo XIII—along with at least four of his predecessors[133]—repeatedly outlined the "disastrous consequences" of these political systems that are gravely opposed to man and to human nature, even though they claim the opposite:[134]

> We speak of that sect of men who, under various and almost barbarous names, are called socialists, communists ... by a scheme of horrible wickedness, while they seem desirous of caring for the needs and satisfying the desires of all men, they strive to seize and hold in common whatever has been acquired either by lawful inheritance, or by labor of mind and hands, or by thrift.[135]

Pope Leo saw where these ideologies would inevitably lead. While claiming to be concerned about the needs and rights of all people, both communism and socialism violate those very rights in the most extreme ways. Pope Leo's language might seem harsh until we consider what these societies routinely did to their citizens. Communist and socialist regimes—in the twentieth century alone—killed between 85 and 150 million of their own people.[136] This is an extreme example of what Benedict XVI was

---

[132] Leo XIII, *Quod apostolici muneris*, 1.

[133] Pius VI, Pius VII, Leo XII, and Pius IX; see ibid., 3.

[134] Leo XIII, *Quod apostolici muneris*, 9.

[135] Ibid., 1.

[136] A few of the dozens of sources that could be listed: Scott Manning, "Communist Body Count," Historian on the War Path, December 4, 2006, http://www.scottmanning.com/

referring to when he noted that "without truth ... love ... is abused and distorted, to the point where it comes to mean the opposite."[137] Killing 100 million of your own citizens is surely the opposite of love. Love under these types of regimes is abused and distorted in every way.

The Common Good

Thus, in considering the proper role of government we remember the words of Paul VI:

> The political community exists ... for the ... common good ... which [is] its full justification and significance, and the source of its ... legitimacy.[138]

Any political system, then, that does not bring about the common good—the good of its citizens—has lost its justification and legitimacy. John Paul II further noted:

> Pope Leo foresaw the negative consequences—political, social and economic—of the social order proposed by "socialism".... He correctly judged the danger posed to the masses ... in recognizing the evil of a solution which, by appearing to reverse the positions of the poor and the rich, was in reality detrimental to the very people whom

---

content/; John J. Walters, "Communism Killed 94M in 20th Century," March 13, 2013, Reason.com, http://reason.com/blog/; Robin Shepherd, "So, How Many Did Communism Kill?," The Commentator, October 5, 2013, http://www.thecommentator. com/; Stéphane Courtois, Nicolas Werth, Jean-Louis Panné, et al., *The Black Book of Communism*: Crimes, Terror, Repression (Cambridge: Harvard University Press, 1999), p. x.

[137] Benedict XVI, *Caritas in veritate*, 3.

[138] Paul VI, *Gaudium et spes*, 74.

it was meant to help. The remedy would prove worse than the sickness.[139]

He went on to say:

The Socialists encourage the poor man's envy of the rich and strive to do away with private property, contending that individual possessions should become the common property of all ... but [if] carried into effect, the working man himself would be among the first to suffer.[140]

This truth became evident to all when the Iron Curtain fell. While the leaders of communist and socialist states may lead extravagant lifestyles,[141] their workers have a standard of living far below those in free-market economies.[142] John Paul II, continuing his comments on Pope Leo's encyclical, noted that these statist systems[143] "are moreover emphatically unjust, for they would rob the lawful possessor, [and] distort the functions of the State. The evils caused by the setting up of ... socialism as a State system ... could not be better expressed."[144]

---

[139] John Paul II, *Sollicitudo rei socialis*, 15.

[140] Ibid.

[141] Mark Blunden, "Kim Jong Un's Luxurious 'Seven-Star' Lifestyle of Yachts, Booze and Food," *Huffington Post*, October 17, 2013, http://www.huffingtonpost.com/2013/10/17/kim-jong-un-luxury-seven-star-lifestyle-north-korea_n_4113788.html.

[142] "Poverty, Prostitutes and the Long, Slow Death of the Soviet Union," DailyMail.com, January 1, 2013, http://www.dailymail.co.uk/news/.

[143] According to Merriam-Webster, "statism" is the "concentration of economic controls and planning in the hands of a highly centralized government often extending to government ownership of industry."

[144] John Paul II, *Centesimus annus*, 12.

Governing Requires Prudence

Equal Opportunity for Economic Initiative, Not Outcome

Nothing that is emphatically unjust, that distorts the function of the State and thus causes evil, can serve the common good. These states suppress the rights of those who live under them, including economic rights:

> In today's world ... the right of economic initiative is often suppressed. Yet it is a right which is important not only for the individual but also for the common good. Experience shows us that the denial of this right, or its limitation in the name of an alleged "equality" of everyone in society, diminishes, or in practice absolutely destroys the spirit of initiative.... As a consequence, there arises, not so much a true equality as a "leveling down."[145]

Thus, Catholics are to support economic and political systems that promote economic initiative, because the alternative —leveling down in the name of equality—further hurts those it claims to help:

> In the place of creative initiative there appears passivity, dependence and submission to the bureaucratic apparatus ... [which] puts everyone in a position of almost absolute dependence.... This provokes a sense of frustration or desperation.[146]

The State and Private Property

For these reasons, another key responsibility of the state is to ensure the right to private property. This right is essential for

---

[145] John Paul II, *Sollicitudo rei socialis*, 15.
[146] Ibid.

economic initiative and the Church has always defended its necessity. As John Paul II put it:

> By defining the nature of the socialism … as the suppression of private property, Leo XIII arrived at the crux of the problem.
>
> The role of the State in the economic sector … presupposes sure guarantees of individual freedom and private property.[147]

Pope Leo further insisted that:

> Private ownership, as we have seen, is the natural right of man, and to exercise that right … is not only lawful, but absolutely necessary. "It is lawful," says St. Thomas Aquinas, "for a man to hold private property; and it is also necessary for the carrying on of human existence."[148]

Thus, there may be no greater oxymoron today than that of a "Christian Socialist Party," something that Catholic social teaching would clearly prohibit us from supporting. Although Christian charity does involve a "preferential option for the poor," that option must always be based on true charity, not on false charity or mere sentimentality.

Democracy, Free Markets, and Capitalism

All of this led John Paul II to ask the question: Is democratic capitalism the best social, political, and economic system available?

> Can it perhaps be said that, after the failure of Communism, capitalism is the victorious social system, and that

---

[147] John Paul II, *Centesimus annus*, 12, 48.
[148] Leo XIII, *Rerum novarum*, 22.

capitalism should be the goal of the countries now making efforts to rebuild their economy and society? Is this the model which ought to be proposed ...?[149]

The answer may come as a surprise to many, especially to those who get most of their news from the mainstream media. First, regarding democracy, the Congregation for the Doctrine of the Faith states:

> The Church recognizes that while democracy is the best expression of the direct participation of citizens in political choices, it succeeds only to the extent that it is based on a correct understanding of the human person.[150]

The Church recognizes that democracy is the best expression of the direct participation of citizens in political choices. Yet she insists that democracy succeeds only to the degree that it is based on a correct understanding of the human person — on understanding the very principles we have been considering. John Paul II continued:

> If by "capitalism" is meant an economic system which recognizes the fundamental and positive role of business, the market, private property and the resulting responsibility for the means of production, as well as free human creativity in the economic sector, then the answer is certainly in the affirmative.[151]

---

[149] John Paul II, *Centesimus annus*, 42–43.

[150] Congregation for the Doctrine of the Faith (CDF), *The Participation of Catholics in Political Life*, 3.

[151] John Paul II, *Centesimus annus*, 42–43.

He made it clear that capitalism, defined as a recognition of the positive role of business, of free markets, of private property, and of freedom and creativity in the economic sector, is certainly the goal and model to be pursued. He immediately added:

> It would perhaps be more appropriate to speak of a "business economy," "market economy," or simply "free economy." [152]

John Paul II recognized that the word "capitalism" has an image problem—it has been redefined and vilified to suit the interests of those who profit from an ever-growing welfare state. Thus, we should clarify that what the Church recognizes as the *best expression*, in today's language, is a *democratic free-market economy*, based on the "rule of law" (CCC 1904) and the common good.

In the next chapter we'll look at the dangers inherent in democracy if the rule of law and the common good are overlooked. For now it is enough to note that John Paul II added:

> The Church offers her social teaching as an indispensable and ideal orientation ... which, as already mentioned, recognizes the positive value of the market and of enterprise, but which at the same time points out that these need to be oriented towards the common good. [153]

Pope Francis versus St. Pope John Paul II

At this point you may be wondering how this can be reconciled with the apparent anti-capitalist stance of Pope Francis—an understandable question given headlines like these:

---

[152] Ibid.
[153] Ibid.

Governing Requires Prudence

Pope Francis' Five Most Radical
Statements on Capitalism[154]

Pope Francis's Challenge to Global Capitalism[155]

Pope Slams Capitalism as "New Tyranny"[156]

Pope Francis Attacks Capitalism,
Calls for State Control[157]

Each of these articles, however, got it completely wrong. They, along with every similar article I found, misrepresented key quotes from Pope Francis's Apostolic Exhortation *Evangelii Gaudium* (*The Joy of the Gospel*). Fortunately, we can download the entire exhortation for free from the Vatican website (http://w2.vatican.va), and verify what the pope actually said.

The first thing you'll learn is that, when you do a word search for "capitalism" in this document, it appears exactly *zero* times. Pope Francis did not use the word, even once, in his over 51,400-word exhortation—a surprising fact given the above headlines. Surely if his intention was to make "radical statements" on, to "challenge," to "attack," and to "slam as a new tyranny" capitalism itself, he would have named it at least once. What Francis did slam as a new tyranny were "ideologies that defend the absolute autonomy of the marketplace and financial speculation."[158]

---

[154] Eric Brown, *International Business Times*, November 26, 2013, http://www.ibtimes.com/.

[155] John Cassidy, *New Yorker*, December 3, 2013, http://www.newyorker.com/.

[156] RT.com, November 26 and 28, 2013, https://www.rt.com/.

[157] William Bigelow, Breitbart.com, November 27, 2013, http://www.breitbart.com/.

[158] Pope Francis, *Evangelii gaudium*, 56.

Yet John Paul II warned of these exact same issues in *Centesi-mus annus*—the very document in which he praised capitalism. That's because, although they are very real dangers, they are not inherent in any one particular economic system.

Pope Francis's most frequent economic warning was actu-ally against consumerism—a word that he used four times. In one instance he referred to it as "unbridled consumerism" (which has been misquoted as "unbridled capitalism" in some articles).[159]

According to Merriam-Webster, consumerism, as Pope Francis used it, is "a preoccupation with and an inclination toward the buying of consumer goods." All popes have spoken against this form of consumerism because it is the opposite of love, which is self-giving for the benefit of another. Consumer-ism is the antithesis of love because it focuses on "self-getting for my own pleasure," as if my immediate material comfort and pleasure were all that mattered, rather than focusing on self-giving.

Pope Francis also spoke against the "idolatry of money and a dictatorship of an impersonal economy lacking a truly hu-man purpose."[160] Many would argue that a "dictatorship of an impersonal economy lacking a truly human purpose" is a fitting description of both socialism and communism—and of all statist forms of government.

Again, these are all things that John Paul II warned against even as he spoke favorably of democracy and capitalism and echoed the Congregation for the Doctrine of the Faith:

[159] E.g., "Pope Calls Unbridled Capitalism 'a New Tyranny,'" *Chicago Tribune*, November 26, 2013.
[160] Pope Francis, *Evangelii gaudium*, 55.

Democracy must be based on the true and solid foundation of non-negotiable ethical principles, which are the underpinning of life in society.[161]

The bedrock of those principles is that all people have equal value and worth, having been created in the image and likeness of God, and thus they always deserve to be treated with love, dignity, and respect.

Government Help — Limited, Temporary

Although John Paul II also pointed out that there can be a legitimate need for the State to intervene in times of crisis — even to the point of substituting for the role of the social or private sectors — he further added that "such supplementary interventions ... must be as brief as possible."[162]

He warned against these interventions becoming permanent — thus replacing the proper role of the social and business sectors — and ultimately leading to an excessive growth in "state intervention, to the detriment of both economic and civil freedom."[163]

Unemployment

In applying these principles to the specific problem of unemployment, John Paul II began by noting that the state must work to "restore dignity to work as the free activity of man."[164] Government programs seem to operate in a way that denies the dignity of work and implies that it is somehow demeaning or even that

---

[161] CDF, *The Participation of Catholics in Political Life*, 3.
[162] John Paul II, *Centesimus annus*, 48.
[163] Ibid.
[164] Ibid., 15.

it is a form of punishment. As we saw in chapter 5, it is the lack of work that is demeaning. Thus John Paul II went on to outline the primary responsibility of the state in this regard: "society and the State will both assume responsibility ... for protecting the worker from the nightmare of unemployment."[165]

He then listed two ways governments have historically done this.

1. Through economic policies aimed at ensuring balanced growth and full employment.[166]
2. Through unemployment insurance and retraining programs capable of ensuring a smooth transfer of workers from crisis sectors to those in expansion.[167]

In other words, governments have historically done this by providing the unemployed with the skills and training needed for them to move as quickly as possible into new jobs in the parts of the economy that are growing—and thus in need of new workers. John Paul II warned, however, that:

[The] primary responsibility in overseeing and directing the exercise of human rights in the economic sector belongs not to the state, but to individuals and to the various groups and associations which make up society.

The state could not directly ensure the right to work for all its citizens unless it controlled every aspect of economic life and restricted the free initiative of individuals.[168]

---

[165] Ibid.
[166] Ibid.
[167] Ibid.
[168] John Paul II, *Centesimus annus*, 15.

This, as we've seen, he strongly opposed:

> Rather, the state has a duty to sustain business activities
> by creating conditions, which will ensure job opportuni-
> ties, by stimulating those activities where they are lacking
> or by supporting them in moments of crisis.[169]

Thus, a true measure of how well a government cares for its
citizens is not how many people are dependent on state aid but,
rather, how many of them no longer need that aid.

Freedom and Responsibility — Subsidiarity

All of this leads us to the key principle of subsidiarity — an often-
misunderstood cornerstone of Catholic social teaching. Briefly
put, subsidiarity consists of the following principles:

- ✢ Matters should be handled by the smallest, lowest, or
  least centralized competent authority.[170]
- ✢ Political decisions should be made at the most local level
  possible, rather than by a centralized bureaucracy.[171]
- ✢ Political and social organizations exist for the good
  of the individual, so they should not take over what
  individuals, or small groups of individuals, can do for
  themselves.[172]

---

[169] Ibid., 48.
[170] Don Fier, "The Principle of Subsidiarity and the 'Welfare State,'"
  Homiletic and Pastoral Review (December 2010), posted at Catholic
  Culture.org, https://www.catholicculture.org/culture/library/view.
  cfm?recnum=9533.
[171] Pius XI, *Quadragesima anno*, 184–186.
[172] CCC 1883; John Paul II, *Centesimus annus*, 13; Pius XI, *Quadragesima anno*, 78.

These principles support decentralization.[173] Subsidiarity stands in stark contrast with the centralized control of life and the economy imposed by more authoritarian forms of government — and is the primary, necessary antidote to them.

Subsidiarity versus the Welfare State

The need for this antidote is so critical that John Paul II warned:

> In recent years the range of such [state] intervention has vastly expanded, to the point of creating a new type of State, the so-called "Welfare State" ... dubbed the "Social Assistance State."
>
> Malfunctions and defects in the Social Assistance State are the result of an inadequate understanding of the tasks proper to the State.[174]

After noting that these malfunctions have resulted in harsh criticism of the Welfare or Social Assistance State, he went on to give the solution — a proper understanding of the role of government and of the principle of subsidiarity:

> Here again the principle of subsidiarity must be respected: a community of a higher order should not interfere in the internal life of a community of a lower order, depriving the latter of its functions, but rather should support it in case of need and help to coordinate its activity with the activities of the rest of society, always with a view to the common good.[175]

---

[173] David A. Bosnich, "The Principle of Subsidiarity," *Religion and Liberty* 6, no. 4 (July–August 1996), Acton Institute, http://www.acton.org/.

[174] John Paul II, *Centesimus annus*, 48.

[175] Ibid.

Centralized government should not take over those things that local governments or private entities can, and should, do for themselves. Centralized government should support them in case of need but never supplant or replace them. The pope then warned of the harm done when this principle is violated:

> By intervening directly and depriving society of its responsibility, the Social Assistance State leads to a loss of human energies and an inordinate increase of public agencies, which are dominated more by bureaucratic ways of thinking than by concern for serving their clients, and which are accompanied by an enormous increase in spending.[176]

A loss of human energies, an inordinate increase in public agencies, the dominance of bureaucratic thinking ("overly concerned with procedure at the expense of efficiency or common sense"),[177] which results in enormous spending increases, all without serving the people's needs—does any of this sound familiar?

The U.S. Government's "War on Poverty" shows how this plays out:

> The poverty rate in 1967 was around 14.5%. In September 2014, it was a nearly identical 14.5%. Yet, adjusted for inflation, during that time government spending on anti-poverty programs increased 16 times—1,600%. US taxpayers spent over $22 trillion on antipoverty programs that had no impact on the poverty rate for those 48 years. And the poverty rate in the twenty years prior to the "War

---

[176] Ibid.
[177] Google's definition of "bureaucratic."

on Poverty" had actually dropped 20%, an average of one point a year.[178]

Reciprocity and the Assumption of Responsibility

It is realities like this that led John Paul II to say:

> In fact, it would appear that needs are best understood and satisfied by people who are closest to them and who act as neighbors to those in need.[179]

And Benedict XVI added that:

> A guiding criterion [for charity is the] principle of subsidiarity ... through assumption of responsibility.
>
> By considering reciprocity as the heart of what it is to be a human being, subsidiarity is the most effective antidote against any form of all-encompassing welfare state.[180]

No individual would willingly spend $22 trillion to help people escape poverty if he saw that the spending didn't work. Long before so much money was spent with no effect — and thus wasted — he would put a stop to it. We, as individuals, would insist on finding more effective means for helping the poor people we knew.

But nameless, faceless bureaucracies, spending other people's money, on recipients they don't meet or know, are under no such compulsion. That is yet another reason why, as Catholics, we are

---

[178] Robert Rector and Rachel Sheffield, "The War on Poverty after 50 Years," Heritage Foundation, September 15, 2014, http://www.heritage.org/.

[179] John Paul II, *Centesimus annus*, 48.

[180] Benedict XVI, *Caritas in veritate*, 57.

to support only those political parties and civic programs that act in accordance with the principles of subsidiarity.

While it is true that such financial waste is atrocious, something far worse than just waste has occurred. Money that was legitimately earned by one group of people was taken by the government, in the name of helping others, but to no effect.

Think of all the good that could have been accomplished over those same forty-eight years if that money had been used to remove the root causes of poverty identified in the previous chapter. How different would the poverty situation in the United States be today if (in inflation-adjusted dollars) that more than $468 billion a year—every year for the last forty-eight years—had been used to provide the job and life-skills training needed to enable the poor to permanently escape poverty and to help them to reach their full potential as human beings?

❖

Summary: Governing Requires Prudence

❖ The government's primary tasks include guaranteeing security, helping to ensure the best conditions for economic growth and private-sector job creation, and enacting policies that enable those who earn money to keep their money.

❖ In terms of unemployment, the government has an additional responsibility to help provide job training so that those who have lost jobs in declining sectors of the economy can quickly and smoothly find new ones in growing sectors.

❖ In justice, the money someone earns belongs to them— not to the State, the community, the government, or the Church. To take that money from someone, even the rich, without his express consent and direction, is theft—even if it is taken in the name of helping the poor.

✛ Charity is charity only if it is freely given, as a gift, under no compulsion from the government or any other entity.

✛ The Church has consistently condemned communism and socialism, which, by their very nature, gravely violate citizens' rights.

✛ The Church has spoken favorably of a capitalism that is a democratic, free-market economy, governed by the rule of law, and directed to the common good.

✛ In contrast with the media headlines, Pope Francis and Pope St. John Paul II agree on this.

✛ The Church strongly warns against the malfunctions of both Welfare and Social Assistance States, and the excessive bureaucracies, spending, and loss of human initiative and freedom such malfunctions inevitably lead to.

Truth 8

We Are Responsible for Reflecting
God's Love in Public Life

❖

We get the public officials we deserve. Their virtue — or lack
thereof — is a judgment not only on them, but on us.

—United States Conference of Catholic
Bishops, *Living the Gospel of Life*

When we experience how complicated, messy, and frustrating participation in politics and civil society can be, it's tempting to withdraw from them altogether. Jesus Himself said that His kingdom is not of this world (John 18:36). And the apostles frequently reminded us that this world is not our permanent home and warned us against becoming polluted by it (Heb. 3:14; 1 Pet. 2:11–12; James 1:27).

But Jesus also told us to be salt and light in the world, to be in the world, although not of it, and to act as leaven within it (Matt. 5:13–16; John 17:14; Matt. 13:33). That is, we are to have both a *preserving* and a *leavening* influence within society. Thus, for all but cloistered religious, withdrawal from the world is not a valid option.

Voting—A Moral Obligation

It is in this context that we read the challenge from the U.S. Conference of Catholic Bishops in their 1998 Statement, *Living the Gospel of Life: A Challenge to American Catholics*: "Every voice matters in the public forum. Every vote counts.... We must exercise that power.[181]

The *Catechism of the Catholic Church* goes further in stating: "Co-responsibility for the common good make[s] it morally obligatory ... to exercise the right to vote" (CCC 2240).

Thus, in the end: "We get the public officials we deserve. Their virtue—or lack thereof—is a judgment not only on them, but on us."[182] So our first responsibility is to vote. We aren't allowed to opt out because we can't find the "perfect" candidate or choose not to participate because of the complexities and frustration inherent in the process. We are morally obliged to vote as part of our coresponsibility for the common good.

Patriotism

We are also called upon to be patriotic—to have respect and gratitude for the good things that our country has done and for the sacrifices others have made to enable our country to do those good things. Vatican II expressed it this way: "Citizens must cultivate a generous and loyal spirit of patriotism but without being narrow-minded."[183]

John Paul II elaborated:

---

[181] USCCB, *Living the Gospel of Life: A Challenge to American Catholics*, 33.
[182] Ibid.
[183] Paul VI, *Gaudium et spes*, 75.

Patriotism is love for everything to do with our native land: its history, its traditions, its language, its natural features. It is a love which extends also to the works of our compatriots and the fruits of their genius. Patriotism ... is a love for one's native land that accords rights to all other nations equal to those claimed for one's own. Patriotism, in other words, leads to a properly ordered social love.[184]

St. Josemaría Escrivá, a twentieth-century saint canonized by John Paul II, summed it up this way:

Love your own country: it is a Christian virtue to be patriotic. But if patriotism becomes nationalism, which leads you to look at other people, at other countries, with indifference, with scorn, without Christian charity and justice, then it is a sin.[185]

Thus, we are called to be generous and loyal, to have the Christian virtue of patriotism in such a way that it does not lead to our becoming narrow-minded — to our being indifferent to the rights and the good of other nations.

Beyond Political Parties and Self-Interest

Next the bishops noted that in exercising these duties we must look beyond party politics, even beyond our own self-interest, to that which promotes the common good:

We urge our fellow citizens to *see beyond party politics, to analyze campaign rhetoric critically, and to choose their*

---

[184] John Paul II, *Memory and Identity* (London: Weidenfeld and Nicolson, 2005), 73–75.
[185] St. Josemaría Escrivá, *Furrow* (New York: Scepter, 1987), 315.

political leaders according to principle, not party affiliation or mere self-interest.[186]

But in doing so, in looking beyond self-interest and party politics, in analyzing campaign rhetoric, what principles are we to use? Here again a lack of education has led to confusion and dissension among well-meaning Catholics. The Church divides issues into two distinct categories, each of which requires a different response.

Prudential Judgment

Much of what we citizens are called to evaluate falls under the category of prudential judgment. A full definition of prudential judgment is beyond the scope of this work, but for our purpose it is enough to note that prudential judgment concerns matters on which good people can, and often do, disagree. They involve discerning the best way to accomplish a *good* and to avoid an *evil*. As such, differences in time, place, and circumstances can lead to different conclusions. Catholics are free to debate, and even to disagree on, the best solutions to issues that are prudential in nature.

Not surprisingly, then, some of the most contentious issues we face today are matters of prudential judgment. For example, before he became Pope Benedict XVI, Cardinal Joseph Ratzinger was Prefect of the Congregation for the Doctrine of the Faith. The Congregation's job is to protect and clarify the Church's true teachings. In his role as the head of the Congregation, Cardinal Ratzinger stated:

Not all moral issues have the same moral weight.... For example ... a Catholic [may] be at odds with the Holy

---

[186] USCCB, *Living the Gospel of Life*, 33, emphasis in original.

Father on the application of capital punishment or on the decision to wage war.... There may be a legitimate diversity of opinion even among Catholics about waging war and applying the death penalty.[187]

In other words, Cardinal Ratzinger said that both capital punishment and the question of waging war involve matters of prudential judgment; that these are both matters that good Catholics may disagree on—even with the pope himself.

As the *Catechism* makes clear:

Assuming that the guilty party's identity and responsibility have been fully determined, the traditional teaching of the Church does not exclude recourse to the death penalty. (CCC 2267)

Legitimate defense can be not only a right but a grave duty.... The defense of the common good requires that an unjust aggressor be rendered unable to cause harm. For this reason, those who legitimately hold authority also have the right to use arms to repel aggressors. (CCC 2265)

Cardinal Ratzinger elaborated:

While the Church exhorts civil authorities to seek peace, not war, and to exercise discretion and mercy in imposing punishment on criminals, it may still be permissible to take up arms to repel an aggressor or to have recourse to capital punishment.[188]

---

[187] Cardinal Joseph Ratzinger, *Worthiness to Receive Holy Communion: General Principles* (July 2004), 3, http://www.ewtn.com/library/CURIA/cdfworthycom.HTM.
[188] Ibid.

Thus, it is perfectly conceivable, and morally acceptable, that faithful Catholics could have differing opinions on the question of imposing capital punishment in a specific case or on the waging of a particular war.

In the same letter, however, the cardinal made it clear that there is another category of issues in which no such difference of opinion is morally acceptable — those that involve intrinsic evil.

The *Catechism* identifies intrinsic evil this way:

There are acts which, in and of themselves, independently of circumstances and intentions, are always gravely illicit. (CCC 1756)

There are ... acts that it is always wrong to choose, because their choice entails ... a moral evil. One may not do evil so that good may result from it. (CCC 1761)

This may be the most practical definition of intrinsic evil:

An act that is always bad, always sinful ... in every age, every place, every situation.... There is *no grey area!* ... Acts that are ... always and everywhere and for everybody and for every situation, *sinful* and *never acceptable*.[189]

Obviously, if something is always wrong, always evil, always and in every situation sinful, and never acceptable, there can be no morally defensible difference of opinion regarding it. That is why the Church is so clear as to our responsibility in such cases.

---

[189] "What Is an Intrinsic Evil?" 3, Catholic Parents On Line, http://catholicparents.org/intrinsic-evil/, emphasis in original.

Examples of Intrinsic Evil

Next we need to identify what these intrinsic evils are. Many intrinsic evils been identified within the *Catechism of the Catholic Church* and other Church documents.[190] Some commonly recognized examples include genocide, mutilation, euthanasia, rape, homicide, human cloning, and child pornography.

Thankfully many of these issues are not relevant in our discussion of politics and society because there is no "Pro-Rape, Pro-Genocide, Pro-Mutilation" party in the United States (at least not at the time of this writing).

There are, however, some items — that are both intrinsically evil and that involve grave matter (mortal sin) — that *are* in political play. Unfortunately, some political parties and politicians actively propose laws that promote the following intrinsically evil, grave practices:

✛ abortion
✛ embryonic stem cell research
✛ euthanasia
✛ human cloning
✛ homosexual marriage
✛ suppressing religious freedom

Impossible to Vote for or to Promote

The Church has been unambiguous regarding our responsibility in these cases:

---

[190] CCC 2352, 2356, 2357, 2369, 1753; John Paul II, *Veritatis Splendor*, 79–83, 90; John Paul II, *Evangelium vitae*, 73; Congregation for the Doctrine of the Faith, *Considerations Regarding Proposals to Give Legal Recognition to Unions between Homosexual Persons*, 10.

Catholics, in this difficult situation, have the right and
the duty ... a grave and clear obligation, to oppose any
law that attacks human life.... For every Catholic, it is
impossible to promote such laws or to vote for them.[191]

Thus, it is impossible for a Catholic to promote or vote for
laws that legalize abortion, embryonic stem cell research, euthanasia, or human cloning, because each one destroys human life.
The *Catechism* clarifies by adding:

Human life must be ... protected absolutely from the
moment of conception. From the first moment of his existence, a human being must be recognized as having the
rights of a person—among which is the inviolable right
of every innocent being to life. (CCC 2270)

The next paragraph adds:

Since the first century the Church has affirmed the moral
evil of every procured abortion. This teaching has not
changed and remains unchangeable.

You shall not kill the embryo by abortion and shall not
cause the newborn to perish.... Abortion and infanticide
are abominable crimes. (CCC 2271)

John Paul II went on to state:

Abortion and euthanasia are thus crimes which no human law can claim to legitimize. There is no obligation
in conscience to obey such laws; instead there is a grave
and clear obligation to oppose them.[192]

---

[191] CDF, *The Participation of Catholics in Political Life*, 4.
[192] John Paul II, *Evangelium vitae*, 73.

We Are Responsible for Reflecting God's Love

The USCCB further explained:

> Abortion and euthanasia have become preeminent threats to human dignity because they directly attack life itself, the most fundamental human good and the condition for all others. They are committed against those who are weakest and most defenseless, those who are genuinely "the poorest of the poor."[193]

While acknowledging that applying these principles to politics can be daunting, they concluded that:

> The basic principle is simple: *We must begin with a commitment never to intentionally kill, or collude in the killing, of any innocent human life, no matter how broken, unformed, disabled or desperate that life may seem.* In other words, the choice of certain ways of acting is *always and radically* incompatible with the love of God and the dignity of the human person created in His image.[194]

This is true even when those involved don't recognize the truth:

> Direct abortion is never a morally tolerable option. It is always a grave act of violence against a woman and her unborn child. This is so even when a woman does not see the truth.[195]

In regard to euthanasia and assisted suicide they added:

> Euthanasia and assisted suicide are *never* acceptable acts of mercy. They *always* gravely exploit the suffering and

---

[193] USCCB, *Living the Gospel of Life*, 5.
[194] Ibid., 21, emphasis in original.
[195] Ibid.

desperate, extinguishing life in the name of the "quality of life" itself.[196]

For as the *Catechism* explains:

> Whatever its motives and means ... euthanasia ... constitutes a murder gravely contrary to the dignity of the human person ... this murderous act ... must always be forbidden and excluded. (CCC 2277)

Again, John Paul II clearly outlined why, as a matter of love, we must stand up for those who cannot stand up for themselves:

> While it is true that the taking of life not yet born or in its final stages is sometimes marked by a mistaken sense of altruism and human compassion, it ... betrays a completely individualistic concept of freedom, which ends up by becoming the freedom of "the strong" against the weak who have no choice but to submit.[197]

Thus, the Church is clear that we cannot support, promote, or vote for laws that legalize abortion, embryonic stem cell research, euthanasia, or human cloning because they each destroy innocent life and go against the love and dignity of the person. Even when those involved in these practices don't understand this or think that some other perceived right trumps these, the deliberate taking of innocent, defenseless life is never acceptable. It is always a crime of the strong against the weak, of the empowered against the powerless, of those who have a voice against those who do not.

[196] USCCB, *Living the Gospel of Life*, 21, emphasis in original.
[197] John Paul II, *Evangelium vitae*, 19.

The Question of "Homosexual Marriage"

While nearly everyone who considers the above cases can see the consistency and reasoning behind the Church's teachings (even if they disagree with them), many wonder why the Church takes such a strong stance against "homosexual marriage." The answer resides in the same principles of love and dignity.

You'll recall from earlier chapters these truths about love:

✣ Love is self-giving for the benefit of another — it is kind, not self-seeking, and always protects the other (John 15:13; 1 Cor. 13:4–7; see chapter 1).

✣ Married love, in the image of the Trinity, must have the potential to generate new life (chapter 2).

✣ "To love someone is to desire that person's good and to take effective steps to secure it"[198] (chapter 5).

Homosexual Activity and the Good of the Other

Again, while a full treatment of the nature, effects, causalities, and correlations of homosexual activity is beyond the scope of this work, the following statistics serve to highlight the rationale behind the Church's teaching. According to the U.S. Centers for Disease Control and Prevention:[199]

✣ There are approximately 50,000 new HIV infections a year in the United States, a rate that has remained unchanged since the mid-1990s.

✣ Nearly two-thirds of these new HIV infections occur among gay and bisexual men.

---

[198] Benedict XVI, *Caritas in veritate*, 7.

[199] Centers for Disease Control and Prevention, *New HIV Infections in the US, 2010*, http://www.cdc.gov/actagainstaids/campaigns/ hivtreatmentworks/resources/infographics.html.

✢ Twenty-six percent of all new infections are among young people ages 13 to 24 (equaling approximately 13,000 new infections among them each year).

The statistics provided by the Canadian GLB (Gay, Lesbian, and Bisexual) lobby are even more distressing. In a 2009 complaint filed against the Canadian health-care system, they noted that their members have:

✢ a higher risk of lung, liver, head, throat, and neck cancers[200]

✢ a rate of severe depression that is 1.8 to 3 times higher than the general population's[201]

✢ a suicide rate that is 3 to 14 times higher than the general population, noting that 30 percent of all suicides in Canada were among the GLB population[202]

✢ a higher risk of anal cancer for GLB men[203]

✢ a higher risk of cervical and breast cancers for GLB women[204]

✢ a life expectancy that is 20 years shorter than average for men[205]

✢ a life expectancy is also lower than average for women[206]

---

[200] Gay, Lesbian and Bisexual Activists of Canada, *Human Rights Complaint against the Government of Canada*, February 2009, p. 5, http://catholicbridge.com/downloads/human_rights_complaint.pdf.

[201] Ibid., p. 4.

[202] Ibid., p. 3.

[203] Ibid., p. 5.

[204] Ibid.

[205] Ibid., p. 3.

[206] Ibid.

These Canadian statistics are used because they were compiled by the GLB community itself and because Canada began legalizing "homosexual marriage" in 2003, making it legal nationwide in 2005,[207] nearly half a decade before the above complaint was lodged.

If love is seeking the good of the other, if it is both desiring and actively taking steps to secure that good, and if it always seeks to protect the one loved, how can promoting a lifestyle that leads to such emotional and physical devastation be *love*? If any other activity led to such a significant decrease in the quality and length of life as homosexual activity does, preventing it would be the top public health priority.

For example, consider driver safety. According to the National Highway and Transportation Safety Association and the Cohen Children's Medical Center:

- There are approximately 32,000 motor vehicle deaths a year in the United States, a number that has dropped by nearly 25 percent since the mid-1990s.[208]
- More than 3,000 U.S. teens die each year in crashes caused by texting while driving.[209] (Therefore, a young

---

[207] Peter W. Hogg, "Canada: The Constitution and Same-Sex Marriage," *International Journal of Constitutional Law* 4, no. 4 (October 2006): 712–721, http://icon.oxfordjournals.org/content/4/4/712.full.

[208] National Highway Traffic Safety Administration, *Fatality Analysis Reporting System (FARS) Encyclopedia*, http://www-fars.nhtsa.dot.gov/Main/index.aspx.

[209] Delthia Ricks, "Texting While Driving Now Leading Cause of Death for Teen Drivers," *Newsday*, May 8, 2013, http://www.newsday.com/.

person is 433 percent *more* likely to contract HIV than to die while texting and driving).

So why is so much more money and effort devoted to teen driving—which poses a much smaller risk—than on campaigns targeting the far greater life-threatening dangers of homosexual activity?

In sincerely caring about the lives and dignity of those who experience same-sex attraction, the Church insists on warning them about the dangers of acting on those attractions. In caring for their dignity, she insists that they be told the truth, regardless of how that truth may be mischaracterized by others or of the negative political repercussions she may experience as a result. For as the Congregation for the Doctrine of the Faith noted:

> Even when the practice of homosexuality may seriously threaten the lives and well-being of a large number of people, its advocates remain undeterred and refuse to consider the magnitude of the risks involved. The Church can never be so callous.[210]

It should also be borne in mind that the Church is not primarily or solely interested in health and physical welfare, but in truth and people's eternal happiness. The Church's attitude toward homosexual behavior starts from God's plan for man, as explained in the first two chapters.

Is Heterosexual Marriage Any Better?

We've seen the devastating impact of homosexual activity on those who engage in it, but is heterosexual marriage any better?

---

[210] CDF, *On the Pastoral Care of Homosexual Persons*, 9.

We Are Responsible for Reflecting God's Love

With rising divorce rates and the apparent disintegration of the nuclear family, is the Catholic Church's teaching on marriage—marriage being a lifelong monogamous relationship between one man and one woman—any better at producing health and happiness? If what we discovered in chapters 1 and 2 about the nature of man and woman in the image of God is true, we would expect the answer to be yes, but what have researchers found?

Numerous studies over several decades have consistently found that the answer is yes—marriage is much better at producing both health and happiness. Consider these findings:

✛ Marital status is one of the most important predictors of happiness.[211]

✛ According to the most recent data, 40 percent of married people said they are very happy with their lives compared with only 25 percent of those who were cohabiting, 18 percent of those who were divorced, and 15 percent those who are separated.[212]

✛ Married people have lower levels of depression than unmarried and report being very happy with their lives at rates almost twice as high.[213]

✛ Divorced people are up to three times more likely to commit suicide than those who are married.[214]

[211] Linda J. Waite and Maggie Gallagher, *The Case for Marriage: Why Married People Are Happier, Healthier and Better Off Financially*, Kindle ed. (New York: Random House, 2002).
[212] Ibid.
[213] Ibid.
[214] Ibid.

✢ Compared with married people, the nonmarried … have higher rates of mortality than the married: about 50 percent higher among women and 250 percent higher among men.[215]

✢ In terms of divorce, those who follow the Church's teachings on sexuality are 10 times less likely to divorce than those who do not.[216]

Married Love and the Possibility of Generating New Life

Finally, we saw that married love, created in the image of God, must contain the potential to generate new life — to "be fruitful and multiply" (Gen. 1:28).

Instead, homosexual activity both shortens the lives of those who participate in it and lowers their emotional and physical well-being. It has never led to the creation of a new life and is physiologically incapable of doing so. Thus the Church cannot recognize it as "marriage."

Does the Church Condemn Homosexuals?

While grieving over the negative consequences to those who engage in homosexual activity, the Church continues to use love as the defining criteria for our treatment of them. Consider these words from the Catechism of the Catholic Church, no. 2358:

---

[215] Catherine E. Ross, John Mirowsky, and Karen Goldsteen, "The Impact of the Family on Health: Decade in Review," Journal of Marriage and the Family 52 (1990): 1061.

[216] Denise Hunnell, M.D., "Natural Family Planning Builds a Culture of Life," LifeNews.com, July 25, 2012, http://www.lifenews. com/2012/07/25/natural-family-planning-builds-a-culture- of-life/.

The number of men and women who have deep-seated homosexual tendencies is not negligible.... They must be accepted with respect, compassion, and sensitivity. Every sign of unjust discrimination in their regard should be avoided.

The Congregation for the Doctrine of the Faith adds:

It is deplorable that homosexual persons have been and are the object of violent malice in speech or in action. Such treatment deserves condemnation from the Church's pastors wherever it occurs. It reveals a kind of disregard for others which endangers the most fundamental principles of a healthy society. The intrinsic dignity of each person must always be respected in word, in action and in law.

An authentic pastoral program will assist homosexual persons ... without deluding them or isolating them.[217]

Finally in this regard, the USCCB notes:

The Church does not teach that the experience of homosexual attraction is in itself sinful.

It is crucially important to understand that saying a person has a particular inclination that is disordered is not to say that the person as a whole is disordered. Nor does it mean that one has been rejected by God or the Church.

While the particular inclination to homosexual acts is disordered, the person retains his or her intrinsic human dignity and value.

[217] CDF, *The Pastoral Care of Homosexual Persons*, 10, 15.

One way in which the Church can aid persons with a homosexual inclination is by nurturing the bonds of friendship.

The local Church community is ... a place where the person with a homosexual inclination should experience friendship.

In fact, the Church actively asserts and promotes the intrinsic dignity of every person. As human persons, persons with a homosexual inclination have the same basic rights as all people, including the right to be treated with dignity.

Church policies should explicitly reject unjust discrimination and harassment of any persons, including those with a homosexual inclination.

Pastoral support should include care for people who become ill with sexually transmitted diseases, including HIV/AIDS.[218]

Thus, rather than condemning persons with homosexual tendencies, the Church insists that they be treated with dignity, care, compassion, sensitivity, and friendship—and that they be afforded the same rights as everyone else, as people created in God's image and dearly loved by Him.

What About Discrimination against Homosexuals?

As we saw, the Church "explicitly reject[s] unjust discrimination and harassment of ... those with a homosexual inclination."

---

[218] USCCB, *Ministry to Persons with a Homosexual Inclination: Guidelines for Pastoral Care*, 11, 13, 23, 29, 38.

We Are Responsible for Reflecting God's Love

Nothing in Catholic teaching serves to justify discrimination against homosexuals in terms of, for example, providing them with basic services or products in the normal course of business.

The Church also recognizes, however, that there is a significant difference between providing basic goods and services to someone that we disagree with and being forced to participate in an event that promotes what we disagree with.

Thus, the Church would strongly oppose refusing to serve a customer, for example, just because he is homosexual. However, the Church would just as strongly oppose forcing someone to participate in an event that promoted things in opposition to his religious beliefs. Thus, she would oppose any law that would force a Muslim or a Jewish caterer, for example, to serve pork, or a Catholic photographer to attend a "homosexual wedding." The government has no right to compel someone to attend, or to participate in, an event that, by its very nature, opposes his religious beliefs.

The same principle holds true with regard to hiring. The Church opposes discrimination against applicants based on race, gender, or sexual orientation, for example, in jobs that are not directly related to these things. Yet, in complete consistency, she would be against forcing an organization to hire someone who was opposed to the very purposes of that organization. She would be opposed to forcing the NAACP to hire a member of the KKK, or a childcare center to hire a pedophile, or a Democratic election committee to hire a Republican operative to run a campaign, or a homosexual-rights advocacy group to hire an orthodox Muslim, or PETA to hire a cattle rancher, or a religious school to hire an avowed atheist, and so forth. The state has no right to compel people to pay others to oppose their own legal interests.

Nowhere is this truer than in cases involving religious freedom, which is why it is specifically protected in the *First* Amendment of the U.S. Constitution. The same amendment that protects freedom of association also applies in the above cases.

Political Parties

Everything we have looked at in the last several chapters makes it clear why the Church, out of love, has said that a Catholic cannot vote for or promote a law that promotes intrinsic evil and that "it is therefore never licit ... 'to take part in a propaganda campaign in favor of such a law, or vote for it.'"[219]

But what does it mean to take part in a propaganda campaign in favor of such a law? What if a political party promotes such a law as part of its official campaign platform? I believe we have the answer to that question in this exhortation by the Congregation for the Doctrine of the Faith:

> In this context, it must be noted also that a well-formed Christian conscience does not permit one to vote for a political program or an individual law, which contradicts the fundamental contents of faith and morals.[220]

By definition, an official party platform is a political program; thus we are also prohibited from supporting it. Just as we cannot support, promote, or vote for a particular law or candidate that promotes such a law, neither are we to support a political party that does.

---

[219] John Paul II, *Evangelium vitae*, 73; Congregation for the Doctrine of the Faith, *Declaration on Procured Abortion*, 22.
[220] CDF, *The Participation of Catholics in Political Life*, 4.

We Are Responsible for Reflecting God's Love

Red Herrings

In considering these issues it is helpful to recall Jesus' instruction to us to be "wise as serpents and innocent as doves" (Matt. 10:16), along with St. Paul's warning not to be taken in by "hollow and deceptive philosophy" (Col. 2:8, NIV). Red herrings are frequently used to confuse people in these areas:

> A red herring is something that misleads or distracts from a relevant or important issue. It may be either a logical fallacy or a literary device that leads readers or audiences towards a false conclusion. A red herring might be intentionally used ... as part of a rhetorical strategy (e.g., in politics), or it could be inadvertent.[221]

Thus, we must be alert and watchful because we know that our "adversary the devil prowls around like a roaring lion seeking some one to devour" (1 Pet. 5:8) and even "disguises himself as an angel of light. So it is not strange if his servants also disguise themselves as servants of righteousness" (2 Cor. 11:14).

The Congregation for the Doctrine of the Faith warned us about this possibility when it noted that "some organizations founded on Catholic principles [have] supported political movements [that are] contrary to the moral and social teaching of the Church" and that some "Catholic periodicals ... have been ambiguous or incorrect, by misinterpreting and ... not taking into consideration the principles mentioned above."[222]

As the USCCB further noted:

---

[221] The Info List, "Red Herring," http://www.theinfolist.com/php/SummaryGet.php?FindGo=Red%20Herring.
[222] CDF, *The Participation of Catholics in Political Life*, 7.

Some Catholic elected officials have adopted the argument that, while they personally oppose evils like abortion, they cannot force their religious views onto the wider society. This is seriously mistaken on several key counts.

First, regarding abortion, the point when human life begins is not a religious belief but a scientific fact—a fact on which there is clear agreement even among leading abortion advocates.

Second, the sanctity of human life is not merely Catholic doctrine but part of humanity's global ethical heritage and our nation's founding principle.

Finally, democracy is not served by silence. Most Americans would recognize the contradiction in the statement, "While I am personally opposed to slavery or racism or sexism I cannot force my personal view on the rest of society." *Real pluralism depends on people of conviction struggling vigorously to advance their beliefs by every ethical and legal means at their disposal.*[223]

Thus, we are warned not to be deceived by misleading arguments, especially when they are presented under the guise of compassion or freedom.

You Can't Legislate Morality

Another red herring is the notion that "you can't legislate morality." At first it may sound wise, but on investigation it proves to be ludicrous. Nearly every law does precisely that. Laws against

---

[223] USCCB, *Living the Gospel of Life: A Challenge to American Catholics*, 24, emphasis in original.

theft, murder, rape, perjury, racial discrimination, incest, slavery, and assault all legislate morality, yet without protest. In practice, people who say, "You can't legislate morality" are generally using it as a mantra to oppose laws against things they happen to support.

This shouldn't surprise us, for as Cardinal Ratzinger pointed out, "anything that does not meet with opposition has obviously not dealt at all with the urgent needs of its time."[224]

No Clear Choice

This red herring argues that, when there is no "perfect" candidate on these issues, we are free to choose whichever one we like most. As an example, a few election cycles ago, an acquaintance mentioned that she wasn't certain whom to vote for in a particular election because both candidates favored abortion. She liked the first candidate's economic policies more, so she thought she might vote for him. However, the first candidate favored completely unrestricted access to abortion in all circumstances—funded by taxpayers—while the second was opposed to abortion in all cases except those involving rape, incest, and danger to the life of the mother.

These are not equivalent options, and the Church is clear in such cases. We have a moral obligation to support the candidate who would do the most good and prevent the most harm—in this case, the second candidate. The same principle holds true in terms of specific laws:

> When it is not possible to overturn or completely abrogate a pro-abortion law, an elected official, whose absolute

[224] Ratzinger, *Gospel, Catechesis, Catechism*, pp. 36–37.

personal opposition to procured abortion was well known, could licitly support proposals aimed at limiting the harm done by such a law and at lessening its negative consequences.... This [is] a legitimate and proper attempt to limit its evil aspects.[225]

In other words, when no candidate (or law) perfectly matches the Church's teachings on these issues, we are obligated to support the one that comes closest to doing so:

It is a question of the lay Catholic's duty to be morally coherent.... There cannot be two parallel lives in their existence: on the one hand, the so-called "spiritual life," with its values and demands; and on the other, the so-called "secular" life, that is, life in a family, at work, in social responsibilities, in the responsibilities of public life and in culture.[226]

Giving Scandal

A final consideration is the potential for causing scandal. Contrary to public perception, causing scandal is a very serious, grave issue. The *Catechism* defines scandal as "an attitude or behavior which leads another to do evil. The person who gives scandal becomes his neighbor's tempter.... Scandal is a grave offense" (CCC 2284).

It further notes:

Scandal can be provoked by laws or institutions, by fashion or opinion.

---

[225] John Paul II, *Evangelium vitae*, 73.
[226] CDF, *The Participation of Catholics in Political Life*, 6.

Therefore, they are guilty of scandal who establish laws or social structures leading to the decline of morals and the corruption of religious practice, or to "social conditions that, intentionally or not, make Christian conduct and obedience to the Commandments difficult and practically impossible [Cf. Eph 6:4; Col 3:21]." (CCC 2286)

It goes on to warn:

Anyone who uses the power at his disposal in such a way that it leads others to do wrong becomes guilty of scandal and responsible for the evil that he has directly or indirectly encouraged. (CCC 2287)

In a democracy, the power at our disposal includes the power to vote and to promote various candidates or parties — to put up yard signs and use bumper stickers, to volunteer our time, to make financial donations, and so forth, and, as already noted, we, along with:

those who are directly involved in lawmaking bodies have a *grave and clear obligation to oppose* any law that attacks human life.... For every Catholic, it is impossible to promote such laws or to vote for them.[227]

A Warning about Democracy

The Church has spoken positively about free-market democracy but has also issued clear warnings regarding its misuse. The Congregation for the Doctrine of the Faith noted: "Democracy must be based on the true and solid foundation of

---

[227] CDF, *The Participation of Catholics in Political Life*, 4, emphasis in original.

non-negotiable ethical principles, which are the underpinning of life in society."[228]

And the USCCB warned:

Democracy is not a substitute for morality.... Its value stands—or falls—with the values which it embodies and promotes. Only tireless promotion of the truth about the human person can infuse democracy with the right values. This is what Jesus meant when He asked us to be leaven in society.[229]

John Paul II shared his concerns more forcefully when he noted:

There is an even more profound aspect which needs to be emphasized: freedom negates and destroys itself, and ... lead[s] to the destruction of others, when it no longer recognizes and respects ... the truth. At that point, everything is negotiable, everything is open to bargaining: even the first of the fundamental rights, the right to life.

The democratic ideal, which is only truly such when it acknowledges and safeguards the dignity of every human person, is betrayed in its very foundations.

This is what is happening [in] ... politics and government.... In this way democracy ... moves towards ... totalitarianism. The state is ... transformed into a tyrant state, which arrogates to itself the right to dispose ... of the weakest and most defenseless members, from the

---

[228] Ibid., 3.
[229] USCCB, *Living the Gospel of Life*, 25.

unborn child to the elderly, in the name of a public interest, which is really nothing but the interest of one part.[230]

Two decades ago John Paul II forewarned that, when a democracy is no longer based on truth, it would inevitably become despotic—when it no longer holds to foundational principles such as this one from the Declaration of Independence: "We hold these truths to be self-evident, that all men are created equal, that they are endowed by their Creator with certain unalienable Rights, that among these are life, liberty and the pursuit of happiness." It would cease to protect the weakest members of its society and eventually move toward totalitarianism. The events of the last twenty years have proven him right.

We began this chapter with the USCCB's challenge: "We get the public officials we deserve. Their virtue—or lack thereof—is a judgment not only on them, but on us." And we've concluded with St. John Paul II's warning regarding what those officials would inevitably become—totalitarians who negate freedom and ultimately destroy life and democracy itself—if we fail to exercise our Catholic responsibility within politics and society. His warning is so dire that it's hard to understand how anyone could ignore it.

The USCCB summed up the challenges and the solution well when it noted:

Today, Catholics risk cooperating in a false pluralism. Secular society will allow believers to have whatever moral convictions they please—as long as they keep them ... private.

---

[230] John Paul II, *Evangelium vitae*, 20.

American Catholics have long sought to assimilate into US cultural life. But, in assimilating, we have too often been digested. We have been changed by our culture too much, and we have changed it not enough. If we are leaven, we must bring to our culture the whole Gospel, which is a Gospel of life and joy.[231]

❖

Summary: We Are Responsible for Reflecting God's Love

❖ Coresponsibility for the common good morally obligates us to participate in politics and society by voting and by being patriotic.

❖ We have total freedom to vote according to our well-formed consciences in questions involving prudential judgments and are free to disagree with each other, and even the pope, on them.

❖ We have a completely different responsibility regarding issues that involve grave matter and are intrinsically evil.

> We cannot promote, support, or vote for them.

> And we cannot support parties or candidates who do.

❖ Such issues currently in political play within the United States include abortion, euthanasia, human cloning, embryonic stem cell research, and "homosexual marriage." We cannot support these because each always involves a grave act of violence of the strong against the weak, by those with a voice against those who have

---

[231] USCCB, *Living the Gospel of Life*, 24.

We Are Responsible for Reflecting God's Love

none, and against the most defenseless in society—even when those involved don't realize this to be so.

✛ Out of genuine love and concern, we cannot support "homosexual marriage" because of the detrimental emotional and physical consequences it has on those who practice it—it contradicts the deepest truths about human nature—and because it is not marriage, as it both shortens the lifespan of those who participate in it and lacks even the possibility of generating new life.

✛ Failure to follow the political and social principles above can lead to the grave sin of scandal—in which we become morally responsible for the resulting sin of others.

✛ Democracy, when not based on the truth of the human person, degenerates into totalitarianism and to the loss of the freedom, protection, and dignity of its people.

Conclusion

Knowing Love

The only thing that counts is
faith expressing itself through love.

—Galatians 5:6, NIV

If what I hinted at in the first chapter of this book is true — that *Everything I Really Need to Know in Life I Learned in the First Three Chapters of Genesis* — then providing a summary of what we've seen thus far should not be too difficult.

In our introduction we asked two fundamental questions: (1) What is God like? (2) What does He think of us? As we sought to answer these questions we learned that:

1. God is a "We":
   ✛ a relationship
   ✛ a communion of Persons
   ✛ a relationship of love so substantive that it is a person — the Holy Spirit — who *is* the love between the Father and the Son

   "God is one but not solitary." (CCC 254)

2. Thus, man, created in God's image, is a "they":
  ✣ a relationship—male and female
  ✣ a communion of persons—husband and wife
  ✣ a relationship of love so substantive that it becomes a
    person—a child—who is the "personification" of the
    love between the spouses

> *"Man becomes the image of God not so much*
> *in the moment of solitude as in the*
> *moment of communion." (John Paul II)*

3. Thus, God invites us to enter into His "We," to enter into:
  ✣ a relationship
  ✣ a familial relationship
  ✣ a familial relationship of love that is a personal, inti-
    mate, friendship with Him

> *"All I want is an intimate friendship with you, . . . You are*
> *everything to me: brother, co-heir, friend, and associate."*
> *(Jesus as paraphrased by St. John Chrysostom)*

4. We then saw that the first thing God did in Scripture was to
work, out of love, for our benefit.
  ✣ Thus, He calls us, in His image, to join Him in the
    ongoing *work* of creation.
  ✣ Work is a gift from God that is essential to our develop-
    ment as human beings.
  ✣ It is a practical way for us to love our fellow man, so to
    deny others the opportunity to work is a serious form of
    discrimination, while to choose not to work ourselves
    is a denial of the image of God within us.

Knowing Love

*"The knowledge that by means of work man shares
in the work of creation constitutes the most profound motive for undertaking it." (John Paul II)*

5. Charity is another requisite expression of love.
    ✣ Thus, in order to live the image of God, we must prac-
    tice charity.
    ✣ A requirement of charity is that it bring about the true
    good of the other person and that it effectively address
    the underlying causes of his condition.
    ✣ Charity must be freely given—coerced giving is not a
    true self-gift and is thus not charity.

*"To love someone is to desire that person's good and to
take effective steps to secure it." (Benedict XVI)*

6. Catholic social teaching tells us that charity must be based
on truth—the truth about God and the truth about man and
his situation.
    ✣ Thus, a one-size-fits-all approach can have serious, un-
    intended consequences. For example, first- and third-
    world poverties are typically very different. Obesity
    and its related diseases are the number-one health
    problem among the poor within the United States.
    Starvation and malnutrition, on the other hand, are
    the number-one health problem among the poor in
    the Third World. These starkly contrasting realities
    call for radically different solutions.
    ✣ The pinnacle of Catholic charity is always to address
    man's most important need—his spiritual need for an
    intimate relationship with God.

*"Without truth, charity degenerates into
sentimentality. Love becomes an empty shell,
to be filled in an arbitrary way. In a culture
without truth, this is the fatal risk facing love. It falls
prey to ... subjective emotions and opinions, the
word 'love' is abused and distorted, to the point where
it comes to mean the opposite."* (Benedict XVI)

7. The proper role of government, then, is to support and create conditions under which man can both work and freely choose to make a gift of the fruits of his labor, for the benefit of others.

+ Thus, government's primary tasks include guaranteeing security, helping to ensure the best conditions for economic growth and private-sector job creation, and enacting policies that enable those who earn money to keep their money.

+ The Church has consistently condemned communism and socialism, which, by their very nature, gravely violate the rights of their citizens. She has spoken favorably of a capitalism that is a democratic, free-market economy, governed by the rule of law, and directed to the common good.

+ The Church strongly warns against the malfunctions of both Welfare and Social Assistance States, and the excessive bureaucracies, spending, and loss of human initiative and freedom they inevitably lead to.

"The principal task of the state is to guarantee ... security, so that those who work and produce can enjoy the fruits of their labors and thus feel encouraged to work efficiently and honestly." (John Paul II)

8. Our responsibility in society and politics, then, is actively to support those candidates, parties, and policies that promote the above.

  ✤ Coresponsibility for the common good makes it morally obligatory for us to participate in politics and society by both voting and being patriotic.

  ✤ We have total freedom to vote according to our well-formed consciences in questions involving *prudential judgments*, and are free to disagree with each other, and even with the pope, on them.

  ✤ We have a completely different responsibility regarding issues that involve grave matter and that are intrinsically evil: we cannot promote, support, or vote for them, and we cannot support parties or candidates who do. Such issues currently in play politically within the United States include abortion, euthanasia, human cloning, and embryonic stem cell research. We cannot support these because each always involves a grave act of violence of the strong against the weak, by those with a voice against those who have none, and against the most defenseless in society—even when those involved don't realize this to be so.

  ✤ Equally we cannot support homosexual practices or "homosexual marriage" because they are intrinsically incapable of generating new life and instead cause great physical and psychological harm to those who engage in them.

  ✤ Democracy, when not based on the truth of the human person, degenerates into totalitarianism and to the loss of the freedom, protection and dignity of its people.

"We get the public officials we deserve. Their virtue—or lack thereof—is a judgment not only on them, but on us." (USCCB)

Knowing God's Love

A Theory of Everything

If you follow science much, you have likely heard of the elusive Theory of Everything (ToE), a single, all-encompassing theoretical framework of physics that fully explains and links together all physical aspects of the universe. Finding a ToE is one of the major unsolved problems in physics.[232]

In a sense, this book has been an attempt to describe a theological ToE. In other words, to present a single, all-encompassing, coherent framework that fully explains and links together all aspects of the universe—the Ultimate, Foundational Truth of the Universe, if you will:

> God is a "We"—a relationship of love, love that is self-giving and that results in new life. Man is a "they," male and female, whose self-giving love also results in new life—children. Work is that same love applied outside the spousal union and is the first practical way in which we make a sincere gift of ourselves for the good of others. Charity is the next practical way we do the same—we share the fruit of our work with those who, through no fault of their own, cannot work. The government's role is to maximize our ability to do all of the above by providing security, stability, and freedom so that people can work, enjoy the fruit of their work, and freely share that fruit with others. In the end, we get the government we deserve because we reap what we sow. Thus, out of love, we must actively promote and support parties, candidates, and policies that best ensure the above.

---

[232] Katie Silver, "Will We Ever Have a Theory of Everything?", BBC Earth, April 8, 2015, http://www.bbc.com/earth/.

Knowing Love

Relationship—Love

The ultimate, foundational truth of the universe, then, is *relationship*—not just any relationship, but a familial relationship of love. On one of his earliest apostolic visits Pope John Paul II emphasized this as he noted:

> It has been said, in a beautiful and profound way, that our God in his deepest mystery is not a solitude, but a family, since he has in himself fatherhood, sonship and the essence of the family, which is love. This subject of the family is not, therefore, extraneous to the subject of the Holy Spirit.[233]

And Pope Francis recently added that:

> God is a "family" of three Persons who love each other so much as to form a single whole. This "divine family" is not closed in on itself, but is open. It communicates itself in creation and in history and has entered into the world of men to call everyone to form part of it. [234]

This is the case because God, who is the author of everything, is a "We," a communion of persons, the Trinity. Christian theology calls this truth a mystery—something that once known makes complete sense, but that we never could have discovered on our own. We can only know it because God has revealed it to us.

God is love—self-giving for the benefit of another. Made in His image, we are to love God with all our hearts, all our souls, all

---

[233] John Paul II, homily during an apostolic visit to the Dominican Republic, Mexico, and the Bahamas, January 28, 1979.
[234] Pope Francis, Angelus message, May 22, 2016.

our minds, and all our strength—and our neighbor as ourselves. This is the first and greatest of all the commandments (see Matt. 22:38–40 and Luke 10:27).

Thus, as St. John of the Cross put it, "At the evening of life, we will be judged on our love."[235]

Final Thoughts—Applied

As we saw in chapter 2, all sin is ultimately the choice to let trust in God's goodness toward us die in our hearts (see CCC 397). It is failing to believe that He who is love itself truly loves us. Jesus' Passion and death on the Cross—having His beard plucked; having His head crowned with a cap of three- to four-inch-long thorns; being beaten so severely that His nose was broken, His eye swollen shut, and His cheek swollen to nearly twice its normal size; being scourged with 123 lashes by whips that had metal and bone fragments tied to their tips; carrying the Cross to Golgotha, and finally being nailed through both wrists and ankles to the Cross, which ultimately led to a slow, painful death by suffocation—all of this He suffered voluntarily, freely, to show us the full extent of His immeasurably great love for us.

His Passion is the antidote to our lack of trust, and by His grace He calls us to put away childish things (1 Cor. 13:11) and instead to enter into the joy of His salvation (Ps. 51:12) by becoming the people, created in His image, that He has called us to be. It is only by accepting that invitation that we can truly live in "the glorious liberty of the children of God" (Rom. 8:21).

And it begins by our first saying yes to His love—"whoever believes in me will have eternal life" (cf. John 5:24; 6:47)—and

---

[235] St. John of the Cross, *Dichos* 64, as quoted in CCC 1022.

then by our finding ourselves through making a sincere gift of ourselves[236] or, as St. Paul put it:

> The only thing that counts is faith expressing itself through love. (Gal. 5:6, NIV)

---

[236] Paul VI, *Gaudium et spes*, 24.

About the Author

John LaBarbara is the founding principal of the Center for Advanced Leadership Consulting and Catechetics (CALC, Inc.). He has been an adjunct professor of Sacred Scripture and apologetics for the Denver Catholic Biblical and Catechetical Schools since 2007. John also served for nearly five years as the vice president of operations for the Fellowship of Catholic University Students (FOCUS) and continues to work as a leadership consultant for them. Prior to that, John served as senior vice president and chief operating officer for the Augustine Institute, where he designed and launched the institute's widely acclaimed distance education program. In addition, he has served as the chief operating officer and consultant for Endow, a dynamic new Catholic apostolate for women.

John graduated summa cum laude with a degree in Sacred Scripture from Simpson University and went on to study New Testament Greek at Fuller Seminary. He is married to his high school sweetheart, Angela, and together they have five adult children and four grandchildren. John and Angela are adult converts to Catholicism who came into the Church after a three-year study of Church history and the early Church Fathers.

John's passion is practical theology—the study of theology so as to make it useful, applicable, and relevant to everyday life. At the request of his students in the Denver Catholic Biblical School, he created an in-depth, year-long apologetics course in 2012 and has been teaching it there ever since. This book is the fruit of that apologetics course as well as his work as the apologetics editor and contributor to *The Didache Bible with Commentaries Based on the Catechism of the Catholic Church*, published by Midwest Theological Forum and Ignatius Press in 2014.

To contact the author about this book, the apologetics series, speaking engagements, articles, or leadership training seminars for business or parish teams please email: John@CalcInc.com.

Sophia Institute

Sophia Institute is a nonprofit institution that seeks to nurture the spiritual, moral, and cultural life of souls and to spread the Gospel of Christ in conformity with the authentic teachings of the Roman Catholic Church.

Sophia Institute Press fulfills this mission by offering translations, reprints, and new publications that afford readers a rich source of the enduring wisdom of mankind.

Sophia Institute also operates two popular online Catholic resources: CrisisMagazine.com and CatholicExchange.com.

Crisis Magazine provides insightful cultural analysis that arms readers with the arguments necessary for navigating the ideological and theological minefields of the day. *Catholic Exchange* provides world news from a Catholic perspective as well as daily devotionals and articles that will help you to grow in holiness and live a life consistent with the teachings of the Church.

In 2013, Sophia Institute launched Sophia Institute for Teachers to renew and rebuild Catholic culture through service to Catholic education. With the goal of nurturing the spiritual, moral, and cultural life of souls, and an abiding respect for the role and work of teachers, we strive to provide materials and programs that are at once enlightening to the mind and ennobling to the heart; faithful and complete, as well as useful and practical.

Sophia Institute gratefully recognizes the Solidarity Association for preserving and encouraging the growth of our apostolate over the course of many years. Without their generous and timely support, this book would not be in your hands.

www.SophiaInstitute.com
www.CatholicExchange.com
www.CrisisMagazine.com
www.SophiaInstituteforTeachers.org